WHAT OTHERS ARE SAYING

Here's what I know about love: it doesn't keep a safe distance. It shows up. It stays. Matthew and Hannah Efird had 57.5 hours with their son Noah, and they didn't waste a single one trying to protect their hearts. They gave him everything. This book is what happened next. It's not polished. It's not tidy. It's the kind of honesty that grabs you by the collar and won't let go. I didn't want it to end. You won't either.

~**Bob Goff**, New York Times Bestselling Author of *Love Does* and *Everybody, Always*

Unprocessed grief grows, and rarely is anything healthy. Processing grief takes courage and a plan. *Even Though, We Will* provides help for the journey of grief we all take. Matthew Efird is not writing from a distance. He is writing from the middle of it. And what he has built inside these pages is something rare: a book that is genuinely FOR the person who is hurting. When loss hits, one of the most paralyzing questions is simply, what do I do next? Matthew answers that question with honesty, with hope, and with a road map that only someone who has actually walked this road could give you. Grief doesn't ask permission. This book helps you respond when it shows up.

~**Jeff Henderson**, Bestselling Author of *Know What You're FOR* and *What to Do Next*, Executive Director of Leadership Innovation and Strategies, Chick-fil-A

In over three decades of neonatal medicine, I have sat with hundreds of families in the most difficult moments of their lives. Medicine can do a great deal, but there are diagnoses where what a family needs most cannot be found in a chart or a protocol. I was there for Noah's story. I watched Matthew and Hannah navigate those 57.5 hours with a grace and a faith that I have never forgotten. What Matthew has written in *Even Though, We Will* is not theory. It is a lived truth, put into words that will serve grieving families and the medical professionals who care for them for years to come. I recommend this book without reservation.

Grief is one of the most isolating experiences a human being can walk through. Matthew Efird does not offer empty comfort in *Even Though, We Will*. He offers something far more enduring: a theology of suffering tested in the fire of child loss and proven sufficient. What strikes me most is the intentional, practical framework Matthew builds around the gospel. The 'arks' he describes are not inspirational ideas. They are life-on-life tools that a church community can wrap around a grieving family. Every pastor, elder, small group leader, and disciple-maker needs this resource. Matthew and his family have not wasted their suffering. They have let God spend it for the glory of His kingdom, and we are all better for it.

Scripture reminds us that our present sufferings are not worthy to be compared with the glory that is to be revealed. Yet living inside that truth when grief is crushing you is an entirely different matter. *Even Though, We Will* does what the best books on suffering must do: it does not explain away the pain, it reframes it within the purposes of a sovereign and loving God. Matthew shows us that God does not waste our deepest losses. He uses them to shape us, conform us, and ultimately carry us. This book will transform hearts, renew minds, and equip the Church to walk alongside those in the darkest of valleys.

Most books about grief tell you what to feel. This one meets you where you already are and gives you something to grab on to. Matthew Efird's honesty about losing Noah is breathtaking, and the Arks he offers aren't theory; they are lifelines forged in real suffering. I wish every pastor, every NICU nurse, and every grieving parent had a copy of *Even Though, We Will* within arm's reach.

Shards of truth from *Even Though, We Will*, resonate in your soul and echo sacred balm for your tattered heart long after you finish turning the pages. In this painfully honest account of Matthew and Hannah's experience in losing Noah, their precious Trisomy 13 baby, soon after birth, we feel the incredible weight of both their triumph and tragedy, a strange phenomenon in the human emotional dichotomy like joy and pain, hope and despair. This book is a must for those struggling with heartloss of all kinds; those desperately seeking help, hope, and healing. In the author's own words, 'We chose to sacrifice our hearts in honoring Noah's life,' and the Creator of all Things certainly redeems their story through the sharing. I highly recommend this book.

Every pastor will eventually sit across from someone whose world has just collapsed, and most of us won't know what to say. Matthew Efird wrote the book I wish I'd had in those moments. *Even Though, We Will* is equal parts gut-wrenching and deeply practical, a rare combination that will serve grieving families and the communities trying to love them well.

~**Jonathan Almanzar**, CEO Iron Forums, Publisher, Pastor, Founder Chick'nCone

Matthew Efird is the kind of leader I respect: refined by hardship and building something meaningful for others. *Even Though, We Will* is honest and deeply needed for anyone facing or leading through loss. The practical "Arks" make it a resource, not just a story. This is a legacy book, and I'm proud to endorse it.

~**Chris Carneal**, Founder/CEO of Booster, Founder of Virtue Village

I've been around tough people my entire life, but the strength Matthew and Hannah showed through the loss of their son Noah is a different kind of toughness. This book doesn't flinch from the hardest parts of grief, and it doesn't leave you there either. Whether you're the one grieving or the one trying to help, *Even Though, We Will* is a resource you'll come back to again and again.

~**Ovie Mughelli**, NFL Pro Bowl Fullback, Atlanta Falcons

Even Though, We Will is a deeply moving and honest reflection on the pain of losing a newborn son, Noah, written with raw emotion and unwavering faith. Through powerful Scripture and practical truths, it gently guides readers through grief while pointing them to the sustaining presence of God. This book is a meaningful resource for anyone seeking comfort, perspective, and strength in the midst of loss.

~**Dr. Ken Thomas**, President, Connect Ministries, Inc.

Even Though, We Will is a beautifully honest and powerfully God-honoring love story that reflects The Great Love Story! I am inspired and moved to trust God more, believing deeply that what He has done in the Efirds, He wants to do in me. My eyes are wet, my soul is refreshed, and my heart is reminded that His power isn't made perfect in my perceived strength, but rather in my weakness.

~**Barry Lusk**, Joy Hub Co-Founder, Iron Forums Atlanta Director

Even Though, We Will is proof that God always prepares his sons and daughters for sufferings. The loss of a child is unconscionable, but by the grace of God, *Even Though, We Will* depicts a "beauty from ashes" story where faith rests on God's character and his exceeding great and precious promises. In this profound testimony, Matthew shares lessons learned, affirming that "weeping may endure for a night, but joy comes in the morning."

~**Dr. Kelvin J. Cochran**, Former U.S. Fire Administrator, Former Fire Chief of Atlanta, Author of *Facing the Fire*

Matthew Efird has written the book our churches desperately need. As a pastor, I have searched for something to put in the hands of grieving families that is both theologically grounded and deeply personal. *Even Though, We Will* is that resource. It will change the way your congregation walks alongside families in their darkest hours.

~**Nick Vipperman**, Senior Minister, Galilee Christian Church, Author of *Switching Shoes*

If you know someone navigating the heavy terrain of loss, they need a copy of *Even Though, We Will*. By weaving raw, honest emotion with practical steps toward healing, this book serves as a vital roadmap for life's most unimagined trials. Most importantly, it anchors the reader in the truth of Jesus: a Savior who is intimately acquainted with our sorrow and promises to walk beside us through every valley.

~**Nathan Unger**, Campus Pastor, Bethlehem Church

Even Though, We Will is a sacred window into the brief but eternally meaningful life of Noah Clifton Efird and the holy ground of a family's intense grief. Through raw journal entries, deep theological wrestling, and the tender "Arks" that helped carry this family through the floodwaters of loss, this book holds the reader's hand in the place where deep praise and deep lament meet. It is achingly honest, deeply human, and anchored in the quiet, stubborn hope of Christ. You will walk away profoundly changed.

~**Lara Silverman**, Bestselling author of the Christian memoir, *Singing Through Fire: Finding Surprising Joy In Life's Darkest Trials*

As a NICU nurse, I have walked with families through the hardest moments of their lives. I have held babies whose time was measured in hours, not years. *Even Though, We Will* is a deeply honest and tender reflection of a parent's journey through grief and loss. Drawn from journal entries about their son, Noah, whose life was brief but impactful in so many ways. This book delves into the reality of grief while offering gentle reminders that faith, hope and love can coexist within unimaginable sorrow. It is a resource I will recommend to every family I serve.

~**Linda May**, NICU Nurse

Even Though, We Will is a heartfelt story of faith in the face of unimaginable pain. With humility and authenticity, Matthew Efird invites readers to see both the heartbreak and the sustaining grace of God in the midst of loss. The Efird's story reminds readers that even the shortest life can leave a lasting impact, and that hope can still be found as we continue to trust God-*even though*.

~**Kyle Cravens**, Team Leader, FUGE Camps, Lifeway Christian Resources

Even Though, We Will is going to make a difference in SO many lives in the Kingdom. I see it primarily affecting at least two groups - those who are walking through unexpected pain and trauma surrounding the loss of a child AND those who God places around them to listen, to comfort, and to walk along that road with them. However, it goes much deeper than pain and ministry to those in pain. Matthew writes out of such deep faith and yet with incredible practicality - at every step. This is a book all in ministry should read AND put in the hands of every couple that is hurting AND every layperson God calls to walk alongside them.

~**Joe Graham**, Former BCM State Director, Georgia Baptist Mission Board (40 Years)

I have had a front-row seat to Matthew Efird's faith journey since his college years, and nothing has revealed the depth of that faith like the loss of Noah. *Even Though, We Will* is not a theory written from a library. It was forged in a hospital room and a cemetery, and every page carries that weight. Read it slowly. Let it do its work.

~**Franklin Scott**, Senior Campus Minister, UGA BCM (35 Years)

Even Though, We Will is an honest account of finding a faith worth standing on in the wreckage of tragedy. Matthew and Hannah don't tell their story to explain away anyone's pain, they share it so no one has to sit with theirs alone. As someone who walks with families daily, this book is a companion for those in the waves and a guide for those who want to love them well.

~**Brandt Akin**, Pastor, The Journey FBC Lavonia

I was privileged to be the Efirds' pastor when they excitedly shared that their little family would be growing by one. Just a few days later, Matthew called to share that there was a problem with some test results. Sitting with, praying with, crying with, and walking beside this young family over the next few weeks and months provided a window to see into Matthew and Hannah's hearts the True Presence of their Savior in their lives. The words penned in *Even Though, We Will* are full of emotion but never clouded by doubt. The story of Noah's life, written by his father, is painfully and brutally honest yet allows the reader room to insert their own tragedy and share in the comfort of knowing others have travelled similarly painful roads before them and emerged stronger on the other side. The wisdom gleaned from these pages will lead you to a deeper understanding of grief and how irreplaceable faith in Jesus is in times of tragedy. In Luke 6:38, Jesus says, "Give, and it will be given to you, a good measure, pressed down, shaken together and running over will be poured into your lap. For with the measure you use, it will be measured to you." Matthew and Hannah have given a "full measure" of themselves in this book. May the reader be stirred and blessed in the overflow.

~**Rob Bailey**, Pastor, mentor and friend

I highly recommend *Even Though, We Will* by Matthew Efird. His unique and personal perspective on grief brings hope as he and Hannah navigate the loss of their son, Noah. They made room for their faith to grow as they turned their grief to mourning and their mourning to a message of healing and grace.

~**Doug Smith**, lifelong mentor and friend

People need a safe place to grieve after a devastating loss. *Even Though, We Will* is an honest account of the Efird family's journey through the loss of their son, Noah. This book shares their story of building an "ark" of faith and hope when life made no sense, offering comfort to those facing unexplainable challenges in their lives.

In this book, *Even Though, We Will*, my friend Matthew shares his heart in a real and authentic way. As you read through it, you will see that there is no perfect formula for walking through grief and suffering, but God remains faithful through it all. I know that God will use this to work in your heart, just as it did mine.

Grief and loss change us forever, but how do we live as changed people? *Even Though, We Will* offers a beautiful and faith-filled answer to this question. Acknowledging the shared need for grace, Matthew Efird takes us on a journey through the mighty waves of grief by sharing his personal story of loss, wrestling with God, and practical ways of loving other grieving hearts well. Written with raw vulnerability, authentic faith, and true empathy, this book is a trusted companion preparing our hearts "to walk on this side of Goodbye".

Matthew Efird writes about the loss of his son, Noah, with a father's unguarded honesty and a faith tested and proven true. *Even Though, We Will*, doesn't offer easy answers, but something better: real tools, hard-won wisdom, and the quiet reassurance that you are not alone in the waves. Every family walking through child loss deserves a copy of this book.

EVEN THOUGH, WE WILL

EVEN THOUGH, WE WILL

Finding Rest in the Waves of Child Loss and the Practical Arks that Carry Us Through

MATTHEW EFIRD

EVEN THOUGH, WE WILL FOUNDATION

ANCHORS IN THE STORM:

To My Beauty, My Bride, My Best Friend, Hannah

Tragedy revealed the raw depth of your character, and it is a masterpiece of grace, tenderness, and fierce loyalty. Thank you for being my partner in the waves and for loving our family with a strength that inspires me every day. I am proud to be your husband.

For Noah Clifton Efird

You taught us how to find rest in the midst of a storm. Your 57.5 hours on this side of eternity changed our world forever. This book is for you, to honor your strength and ensure that your story continues to point others toward the Savior.

To Walker, Abel, and Warren

My warriors. May you grow up knowing that your brother's absence is not a void, but a testimony of God's faithfulness. You are purposefully designed by our Creator. I can't wait to see what you do in this life. May you become mighty men of God. I am so proud to be your Dad-O.

And for the Grieving Soul

Holding this book with trembling hands. May these pages be an Ark for you when the waves are high. Even though the storm is real, we will still stand.

CONTENTS

THE FOUNDATIONAL GROUND

THE COMMUNITY MANUAL

PREFACE: HOW TO USE THIS BOOK

If you are holding this book, you are likely in the middle of a storm you never asked for, or you are standing on the shore trying to figure out how to help someone you love. Grief is not a sprint; grief is a grueling ultramarathon, and the mental fog that comes with it can even make reading feel like an impossible task.

This book is designed to be your companion in the waves. Here is how it is structured to serve you:

The Waves: Our Story

The first half of this book follows our family's chronological journey with our son, Noah. These chapters are raw and often unedited, taken directly from my journals during our pregnancy, the 57.5 hours with him on this side of heaven, and the months that followed. They are meant to sit with you in the "not okay" moments and remind you that you are not alone in your pain.

The Arks: Practical Passage

At the end of each chapter, you will find a specific "Ark". In the Bible, the Ark wasn't built to take Noah around the flood, but to provide a structure of safety through it. In these pages, an

Ark is a practical takeaway or a foundational truth that helped keep our family afloat.

Internal Arks: Tucked within the stories, you will find Ark call-outs.

They are identified like this:

THE ARK: These are immediate survival tips, such as finding a communication manager for your family or learning to say "no" when your energy is gone, that were vital to our own navigation.

- If you are currently struggling to function: Feel free to jump to the Appendix: List of Arks at the back for a quick reference of these survival principles.

The Foundational Ground

The middle chapters shift from our story to the theological wrestling we did with God. We explore the difficult questions: Why does God allow bad things to happen? How do we find joy when happiness is gone? This section is for when you are ready to find a solid floor to set your table on.

The Manual for Community

Chapters 24 through 29 are specifically for the friends, family, and community members who want to help but don't know what to say. If you are reading this to support a loved one, these chapters provide a clear map for how to display true empathy and love in action.

A Final Note: You do not have to read this in order. If the "fog" is too thick today, just read one Ark. If you need to weep, sit in the story. If you need to fight, look at the theology. This story is offered without expectation, only with the hope that it meets you exactly where you are.

An Invitation to the Ark

This story is a grieving father's humble attempt to share the darkest moments of his life. It is not perfect. It does not fully encapsulate our journey or our family's perspective. This story is told through my eyes, from our family's lived experience. This book is written from the perspective of two parents who follow Jesus Christ. Our faith did not begin with tragedy, but it became the ground we stood on when tragedy came. What you will read is not a formula for healing, nor a universal prescription for grief. It is simply the way we learned to breathe, to hope, and to keep standing.

If you are walking through grief yourself, you may find companionship here. If you are reading to love better someone who is grieving, you may find insight. And if you are uncertain what you believe, you are still welcome here. This story is offered honestly, without expectation, only with the hope that it meets you where you are.

This book has a threefold purpose:

1. *To honor our son, Noah Clifton Efird, and to glorify God in our suffering*

2. *To come alongside grieving individuals and families with compassion and love*

3. *To equip those walking beside grief with wisdom, patience, and empathy*

This is Noah Clifton Efird's story. He lived 57.5 hours on this side of eternity. He was deeply loved and will be forever cherished. Our family has grieved since our doctor told us the news of his diagnosis. We have so many people to thank for their support of our young family.

Foremost, we thank our Lord and Savior, Jesus Christ. This tragedy did not create faith in us but further solidified our desperate need for a Savior. Tragedy exposes character, and the tragedy of the passing of our sweet son, Noah, has torn away so much facade, leaving a raw, tender, transparent love for each other rooted in the perfect Love of our Savior. Without God's presence and mercy, we would not be standing today.

Navigating grief is similar to standing in the waves of a mighty storm. There are more times than not that the waters feel as if they are against you, pulling you out to sea, tossing you around like a rag doll. Waves crash against you. Some days, they knock you to your knees. Some days, they take your feet out from under you and hold you down as wave after wave crashes over you. It is in the midst of this storm that you must rely foremost on your Savior and second on your community.

Writing was and is so therapeutic to me. If we never shared the words that I have journaled, at least I was finding an avenue for processing. This book started as my attempt to process what was going on within our family. Some of the writing was shared via social media as family updates, and we received a lot of encouragement to expand and put it into this format. I originally didn't feel pulled to share these raw words with others, but then I started receiving the words of how God was redeeming our story in the lives of our friends and family through the words we were sharing. Hannah and I prayed together for months about this book. I would write when I had time, sometimes early in the morning and others late into the evening. One of the ways that I process events is by describing them to others. I found it hard to finalize the book for publishing, because it felt that it was closing a chapter in our life that was so brief. Instead, this book is an attempt to describe our family's story with our son, Noah Clifton Efird, and honor his life as we navigate the days until we are reunited.

To the individual or couple in the midst of the deepest grief of your life, we see you, and we are praying over you. This book will challenge you, but don't run from the difficulty. There is purpose and healing for your pain.

To the family member or friend of one deeply grieving, this book will give you an insight into their day-to-day experiences. Don't just force this book on them. Read it, sit with its challenges, and pray for abundant mercy and grace for those whom you love fiercely who are hurting deeply.

To the individual who happens upon this book on the other side of the storm, my prayer is that this book will equip you to better weather the future storms in your life. Likewise, I pray that it helps you process previous hurt in your life.

Our prayer is that this book finds its way into your hands at the appointed time for whatever season you find yourself currently in or heading into. We are not perfect, but we serve a Perfect Savior who has redeemed our mess to display miracles. We pray for you. We pray over you. You are not alone. Tragedy feels isolating, as if you are standing alone. Don't face this storm alone. You will need your community now more than ever. Most importantly, you will need to lean into a relationship with Jesus Christ, finding solid ground in His ever-present Grace and Mercy.

PART ONE

THE WAVES

Our Story

These chapters follow our family's journey from the word that changed everything to the slow, uneven work of learning to live in its wake. The writing is raw. Much of it came directly from journals written in hospital hallways and quiet living rooms.

If the fog is too thick to read right now, turn to the Appendix. Come back here when you are ready.

CHAPTER 1

BEFORE THE WAVES

When one word alters the course of a family.

"*A*bnormalities." That word hit our family like a ton of bricks. It was softly spoken by a new doctor during our regularly scheduled ultrasound appointment. We had no clue that one word would alter the course of our young family.

Hannah and I were high school sweethearts. We had the gift of growing up alongside one another, and we began dating the summer after my senior year. I share this not to paint a perfect picture, but to establish what was at stake when a single word would later alter the course of our family.

I knew early on that I wanted to marry Hannah. She is my beauty, my bride, my best friend. I am so proud to be her husband and to be on this journey together. If you were to Google the definition of a wife and a mom, Hannah's picture should be the only illustration needed: not because she's perfect, but because she loves fiercely and faithfully. I've watched her live out her love for our family in a thousand quiet ways long before grief ever tested us.

She is the quintessential bride you dream of and pray for as your companion, your helpmate, and the mother of your children. We knew early in our marriage that we wanted kids, and we both felt pulled toward a larger family made up of adoption, fostering, and biological children if given the chance. Our friend group started to have kids as we were entering our third year of marriage. We had both been feeling led to start trying, but little did we know it would take nearly two years to become pregnant with our oldest son, Walker.

He was an amazing baby, and he is a precious, tender, extroverted gift from God. He loves people, loves physical touch, and loves to play rough; he takes after me in those ways. His cuteness and compassion come from Hannah. While we were cherishing our time with Walker, we started praying about our family growing, since neither of us felt like we were done as a family. Hannah and I talked about timing and what we thought would be best for our family and for Walker. Naively, I said that anything would be easier than Walker, since we had just opened one of our businesses when he was born. If we could survive that as a couple, we could survive having a baby any time of the year, and nothing would be as difficult as that first year with Walker. Little did we know what was on the horizon for our family.

Hannah and I live outside of Athens, Georgia, close to our alma mater, The University of Georgia (Go Dawgs!). We manage a few businesses and, at the time, served on staff at a local church, Oconee Heights Baptist Church. We love to travel, mainly for the opportunity to eat good, local food. We enjoy hosting friends and watching sports. Our days are spent serving our staff, our customers, our church, and our community. Until September 17, 2019, we held an unhealthy and fragile view of community. We believed in it, taught about it, and encouraged others to lean into it, but we still functioned as if strength meant self-sufficiency and leadership meant carrying weight quietly. We have been very blessed, and both feel that leadership is an area we have been gifted in, and it was precisely that gifting that made us slow to admit we could not make it without help from others. This unhealthy view was self-focused. Being within a community forces you to not just focus on yourself. Our unhealthy view was that we could help but didn't need their help. We could be generous, but didn't need generosity. We could serve, but didn't need serving. We wanted to be needed by others but didn't want to need others.

Tragedy exposes character. We soon found that a recurring flaw was an unrealistic view of community. Community is built on the support of one another. It's a give-and-take relationship. We had pridefully inflated our ability to give and not take within relationships. The strength we would need for this journey would not be found within ourselves, but first in Jesus Christ and then within the bonds of our community. We had told people for years that it was okay to not be okay, but that it wasn't okay to stay that way. For the first time in our marriage, we found ourselves not okay, with no clear idea how to move forward. We were in desperate need of help to navigate the waters between hurting and healing. We believe our areas of hurt can offer a platform to help others, but only after healing takes place. It is easy to avoid processing your hurt by trying to jump into helping.

Don't fall into this trap.

Helping will come, but it can't be at the expense of your own healing, and we will look into this further in Chapter 25: Hurting, Healing, Helping. We intentionally took time away from business and church to spend time together processing, talking, hurting, lamenting, and grieving our son, Noah, who now has a residence in Heaven. He will always be part of our story. While the intensity of the pain will subside at times, it will never fully go away. Just like waves, they come at different intervals and with different intensities. We must not be afraid to engage our pain, for in it we find a place for true healing. Emotions, in and of themselves, are natural. It is what we do with them that is healthy or unhealthy. Don't run from your emotions during your grieving process. Embrace them, feel them, talk about them even when they don't make sense or seem too dark to say out loud. God is not afraid of your feelings. Learn to speak them out loud, as they will lose part of the grip they have on you.

Grief did not come to us as a single moment, but as something far more unpredictable. As we tried to make sense of what we were experiencing, one image kept returning: waves.

In those early days, it felt as though our family was being tossed by a violent storm at sea, bringing a whole new meaning to Noah's Ark. The imagery of the Ark wasn't just a Sunday School story anymore; it became our reality. We named our son Noah, but we quickly realized we also had to build our own 'arks' just to survive the waves that were crashing over us. We didn't need a way *around* the storm; we needed a way *through* it. In this book, I offer several of those "Arks" as practical advice from someone who has weathered the storm. These "Arks" helped our family navigate the waters of grief. Waves and storms come and go, but these truths can be arks for you and your loved ones. We pray they help provide you with passage through your storm.

THE ARK is how each of these truths will be identified.

You may be thinking, "Why an ark?" In the Bible, the ark was a boat-like structure built to provide Noah and his family passage through immense suffering and destruction. Due to the wickedness in the world, God was going to destroy humanity with a flood, but chose to save Noah and his family. Beyond the connection to Noah's name, we found many 'arks' throughout our journey that helped provide our family passage through our immense suffering. Imagine the Biblical Noah and his family sealed inside the ark as the storm began to rise around them, the waters began to swell, and the rain began to beat down. Slowly, the ark was lifted off its platform, and they began to be tossed back and forth during the storm. The destruction was still happening around them, yet the ark provided passage through the storm. As much as I would like to offer a simple response that could remove the suffering from your life, we aren't offered that in scripture, so we won't offer that here either. This distinction between *removal* and *passage* became central to how we understood our grief. Psalm 30:11 is one of the verses that I clung to.

"You turned my wailing into dancing."

Psalm 30:11 NIV

Now I enjoy dancing. This doesn't mean that I am particularly good at it, but a dance party, especially at a wedding, fills my heart to the brim. I would quote this verse over our family almost daily, longing for the days of dancing to return, because I wanted him to turn my wailing into dancing by removing it. There is a rawness in the reality of our lives caused by the brokenness of sin.

As you consider your own journey, let me ask you a question that I've wrestled with. What if the presence of God was not to remove all suffering in our lives but to provide an avenue through it? That question unsettled me, because it challenged everything I wanted God to do for us. The meaning for "turned" in Psalm 30:11 is not a removal but a transformation or conversion. After this revelation, I wrote this declaration in my journal following Noah's memorial service. What follows are the unedited words I wrote in my journal in the days after Noah's memorial service.

It's not a removal of my mourning, but a turning for it. It's a purpose for my pain. It's a slow healing of my wound. It is beauty for my ashes. My wailing has an avenue for processing and healing. I won't always sit in this intense pain, but I shouldn't be afraid of it because it isn't going away. I need to experience this moment so that it can be transformed. In the presence of my Savior, I can find the freedom to dance.

Those words didn't remove the pain, but they gave it language. It's okay to not be okay, but it's not okay for us to stay that way. In the presence of our Savior, we find freedom. Not the freedom of having our struggles magically removed, but freedom to navigate through the struggles and trials in life. That kind of freedom didn't end our grief, but it gave us a way to take the next step.

If we don't come to grips with the reality of suffering in our lives, then when we are met with it, we will feel as if God has abandoned us. Death forces us to focus. Focus dictates direction. To find true healing, the direction you and I go must be into the presence of our Savior. In the midst of your chaos, you may feel abandoned, but you are not. Even when you feel like running, He is right there with you.

There is freedom from sin found in the finished work of Jesus Christ. In the presence of our Savior is freedom. The experience of freedom is directly tied to the strength of the liberator. Our liberator, our Savior, Jesus Christ, had the strength to conquer death. He boldly died on a cross, was laid in a tomb, and rose again three days later to provide an avenue for us to be in the presence of God. His presence doesn't overlook your sorrow, your anxiety, your trials, your hurt, or your questions. His presence provides a way through them. He is Jehovah Shammah, The Lord is There. When we accept Jesus Christ as our Lord and Savior, He will be right there with us, providing freedom and restoration throughout our lives.

From our experience: patience and mercy will not come easily for you as you grieve. Pray earnestly for them. Be quick to accept your faults and ask for forgiveness. The old adage is so true: hurt people hurt people. If you are not careful, you will quickly find yourself hurting the people around you that you care most deeply for. Be slow to speak and quick to listen. As we learned, you will need your community. Don't push your pain onto them; they are already hurting seeing you hurt. In this book, we will use our story to share how we navigated the waters of grief, prayerfully expecting that God will redeem our story for your good and His Glory.

THE ARK: God does not always remove the storm; He provides passage through it.

CHAPTER 2

STANDING TOGETHER

*Fighting for each other when it's easier to fight
with each other.*

For those of you navigating grief together within a marriage, our heart goes out to you. Grief and tragedy can either drive a wedge between you or fuse you together, deepening and strengthening the bond you share. The latter takes dedicated effort, as the former is far easier. Do yourself a favor and commit to fighting *for* each other rather than fighting *with* each other. No matter where you are in your process of grief, today is the day for change, and change is created one day at a time. Be thankful for your spouse, and pray for grace and maturity in yourself to love them well during this season, as they will be critical in helping you move through your grief and emerge stronger together. You will make mistakes. Whether you truly know it or not, you are not perfect, and navigating grief will expose some of the worst parts of you. You will be blessed if your spouse responds to your shortcomings with grace and maturity.

I was immensely blessed as Hannah continually responded with maturity and grace in the midst of my hurt. I worked to keep the Golden Rule: treat others as you want to be treated. Our responses are often confined to our own perspective. By going into the season with the desire to love and respect each other, while allowing our grief to drive us together rather than apart, we just set forth to respond with grace and maturity. Did every conversation go smoothly? Of course not. Did we jump on the 'Crazy Cycle' (a concept from Dr. Emerson Eggerichs we'll dive into later)? Of course, we did. What we learned was not to be defined by our shortcomings, but to fix our eyes on things above. It was reinforced in our lives that focus dictates direction. We chose foremost to focus on Jesus and, secondly, to focus on each other, keeping Walker third and business fourth.

We learned early on in this process that the question, "Is something wrong?" was futile. Of course, something was wrong. We came to the realization that even though we had been together for nearly 10 years, we were going to have to establish ground rules for our communication moving forward. These new ground rules provided space for the other to experience their emotions, and grace when those emotions weren't handled with the poise you might expect from an adult. We created a two-question survey for each other, but it always required one of us to be mature in the moment to use them.

1. *Did I do something to upset you?*
2. *Would you like to talk about how you're feeling?*

These two questions provided such freedom for each of us. I would have days where I just felt "off" from the time my feet hit the ground. Instead of having to put on a face in front of Hannah, I was able to answer the first question with a "*no*" and the second with a "*not right now.*" When I was ready, we would regroup and debrief. Likewise, this helpful practice prevented both of us from walking on eggshells around the other one. Hurt people hurt people. We were both hurting so deeply, so it was easy to react from our place of hurt in a hurtful way. Normally, we address problems head-on in our marriage, bringing to light the issue, talking through the concerns, and apologizing for the wrongdoing. This style works great for our normal life when she or I do something selfish. One of us is the wrongdoer, the other is the receiver of the wrongdoing. We are able to repair the wrong and move through it. But not this time.

Nothing could be fixed, apologized for, and rectified. Instead of doing nothing, we had to do something. So we created our two-question survey to allow each other the space to be hurt and process. The caveat for this practice to work is honesty and the absence of manipulative intent. If you can both work from this place, you can navigate the emotions that are to come. The first question focuses on what you can control. *Have I done something to upset you?* Have your actions caused additional harm to your spouse unknowingly? Remember, hurt people hurt people, so this can easily be a Yes.

Please don't make your spouse read your mind. This kind of behavior is not helpful or edifying in normal circumstances, and it becomes toxic in the midst of grief. We found that asking this question first gave us the framework in which to move forward in the conversation. For instance, when I did something that hurt Hannah, I wanted to correct it as soon as possible. I wanted an opportunity to listen to her, hear why what I did caused her harm, apologize and ask for forgiveness, and then work to rectify the wrong. If she was upset because of something I did, there could be steps to take to fix the issue. If she wasn't upset because of something that I did, then the steps weren't so clear.

A *no* to question one needed to be followed by the second question: *Would you like to talk about how you are feeling?* Once we had clarified that the pain was not caused by the other, we needed to give one another the space to share when it felt comfortable. Many times in those moments, we couldn't put words to our feelings, so trying to discuss them would have been fruitless. Other times, we knew exactly how we felt and could articulate it clearly. This question gave each of us ownership over how we were feeling. I was responsible for how I responded to my emotions, and this subtly reinforced that responsibility for both of us. It also provided the other person with insight into the needs we each had in that moment.

Here's an example of how this played out.

I am harsh when Hannah asks if I can help her by taking the trash out. Hannah, being a very mature Christian woman, asks me question one: *Have I done something to upset you?* I snapped back to reality and realized I had been mean in my response to my Bride. I wasn't mad at her; I was just sad. I had been playing and stacking blocks with Walker, and my mind wandered to all the things I would get to teach him, which then dovetailed into all I would never get to teach Noah. My heart was aching, and I was doing all I could to keep it from tearing apart. Not knowing where my mind was, my Bride, who had been diligently working on dinner, asked for help. Earlier that evening, I had even told her I would be happy to help if she needed me. So, from my place of hurt, I reacted in a way that caused more hurt. This cycle could have continued if Hannah hadn't chosen the mature response. Maybe you've been in conversations like this, where they go on so long you eventually forget what they even started over. Early in our marriage, we were introduced to *Love & Respect* by Dr. Emerson Eggerichs. I cannot recommend it highly enough.

The 'Crazy Cycle' is a concept that explains how a wife's need for love and a husband's need for respect are foundational and interconnected. When a wife feels unloved, she may react without respect; when a husband feels disrespected, he may react without love. In the midst of grief, this cycle can spin out of control before you even realize you're in it. These two questions became our life line. To borrow a phrase from Dr. Eggerichs, question one kept us off the 'Crazy Cycle' in the midst of our grief. I would respond to Hannah's question with a *no*. She would follow up with question two, *Would you like to talk about how you are feeling?* Depending on the circumstances with Walker, normally this would be answered with a quiet, Not right now. Many of these follow-up conversations would happen early mornings, during nap times, or late at night after he was asleep. Navigating grief with a toddler is trying, to say the least.

In this example, Hannah would share that my harsh response was very unloving to her. She was working hard on dinner, and I had even offered to help. She would ask me why I responded that way. I would offer a sincere apology for being rude and explain how my mind had wandered when she asked for my help. It gave me an avenue to share how I was hurting as I thought about the future. She typically shared in those difficult thoughts, and instead of grief driving a wedge between us, grief became something that drove us together. Rather than responding in a way that caused more hurt, she responded with maturity and grace. The situation was diffused, and I was given the opportunity to acknowledge my hurt and the space to heal.

I was given the opportunity to explain myself and ask for forgiveness. We found that these two questions required a lot of us, yet created space for remarkable freedom within our grief, freedom we didn't know was possible.

Not all interactions were a No to question one. A lot of times, we had done something that had hurt the other person, and it needed to be rectified. In our home, we apologize for the wrongdoing and ask for forgiveness from the other person. This acknowledges the ownership of the wrong and allows the other person to extend forgiveness, as it is not immediately guaranteed. We believe that just saying "I'm sorry" falls short of seeking restoration of the relationship.

In this season, a lot of the hurt seemed to be around normal household activities. Hannah would ask me to clean up my stuff after I got home from work, because I have a terrible habit of leaving things in piles, typically by the front door. I sense Hannah is upset with me, and I ask her question 1. Her response is a Yes. Immediately, I clue in and apologize. "Sweetheart, I'm so sorry I've upset you. Will you please share with me what I've done?" After she asks me to pick up for the third time that day, I put away my stuff. Then, I re-engage the conversation. "I'm really sorry that I left my stuff out again. Will you please forgive me?" It seems small, picking up shoes or taking out the trash, but in the midst of a storm, these are the small things that keep the water out of the boat. When we choose to own our faults quickly, we stop the 'Crazy Cycle' before it has a chance to sink us.

If you take nothing else from this book, I pray you adopt these two questions. They have provided such grace and mercy to our relationship. As you become accustomed to asking them, you will find they are a tender way to acknowledge harshness in your spouse.

1. *Did I do something to upset you?*

2. *Would you like to talk about how you're feeling?*

For me, it feels like a gentle hand on my shoulder saying, "Hey, big guy, your words are more damaging at this moment than you realize. Let's take inventory of what's going on internally and change the way we're approaching others." If you are like me, your spouse often knows you better than you know yourself. These questions are a way to gracefully acknowledge shortcomings and allow space to make changes. Hannah and I are good-willed people. We love each other and our boys. We don't want to intentionally hurt each other. We found that these questions put the unintentional hurt on display for the offending party without using a combative approach.

THE ARK: Grief cannot be fixed, but marriage can be protected by choosing unity over winning.

CHAPTER 3

CARRYING THE WEIGHT

*Wading into the murky waters of
a terminal diagnosis.*

Hannah and I had been trying for a few months, praying that God's timing would be perfect for our family and that we would rest in His faithfulness, just as He had been faithful with Walker. I can remember driving home from meetings and hearing Hannah say how tired and sick she was feeling. I slipped and asked over the phone if she was pregnant. (Young men, please do yourself a favor and ask your bride this question in person. Do not put her in the position I put Hannah.) She avoided the question and said she needed to get off the phone to help Walker. When I got home, I gave her a kiss, and she said that Walker had gotten me a surprise at the store. I looked up, and Walker was carrying a "Big Brother" book down the hall. I was beaming with pride, excited for our family to grow. I couldn't wait to see my bride continue to flourish as a mom of multiple children, and so excited to see our sweet son mature into the big brother role. We knew he was going to become an excellent big brother. I am a very vocal and open person (hence the book), and I was so excited to tell everyone. Hannah, in the tenderness of a prompting from the Holy Spirit, felt it was best if we waited to tell people.

We went to our six-week appointment, and there was a heartbeat! We were thrilled. I was ready to tell people. I texted some very close friends so that they could be praying for us, but Hannah still felt as if something was off. We waited to tell people until after our second doctor's appointment. We knew that we were having an ultrasound, so we took Walker to see his younger sibling for the first time! We were talking with the sonographer, sharing how this child was such an answer to prayer. She gently asked if we planned to do genetic testing; her experience already told her what she was looking at, and we said yes. We wanted to prepare ourselves for whatever was to come, but it wouldn't change our approach as parents during the pregnancy itself.

We were so excited to see the heartbeat and the little outline of his body. She politely printed some pictures and helped us to our next room. We waited for what seemed like an eternity, trying to corral our 19-month-old son, who was rapidly growing tired of the toys and the children's stool in the room. Finally, there was a knock at the door, and in walked a new doctor. We were distracted by Walker and the giddiness of being a family of four and didn't notice the somber look on her face. She put her paper down and said that there were some abnormalities on our ultrasound. It was September 17, 2019; our lives would never be the same.

"Abnormalities" rang in my head. In the midst of this news and me trying to focus on the doctor instead of our toddler, Walker decided to jump off the stool and face-planted, bursting his lip. Blood went everywhere, and everyone was now in tears. I heard words like: Trisomy 13. Trisomy 18. Trisomy 21. Translocation. Terminal diagnosis. Genetic testing today. Specialist ASAP. Over 90% of children with his diagnosis don't leave the hospital if they make it to full term alive. I still don't know everything our doctors tried to communicate to us. Hannah cried. Walker cried. I cried. For the first time during this journey, I could feel my body going numb to the pain around me, as if a primal safety mechanism had been activated. I realized how quickly my body was trying to protect me from the pain. My years of training were kicking in.

After we got Walker cleaned up, I held him and paced the room. Hannah asked questions: "What does this mean? Did we do something wrong? Could we have prevented this? Did we cause this? What will happen to our child? Is this definitive?" Then Hannah cried more, and I tried to distract Walker. Walker wanted mommy to hold him, so I handed him over. I asked similar questions: "What does this mean? How do we know for sure? Who do we meet with from here? Is Hannah in danger? Is there anything we can do?" By this time, Walker needed space to move around, and we all needed a change of scenery. We were given our next steps, our doctor left the room, Hannah and I embraced, cried, and prayed that God would heal our son. The first of 1000s of prayers for healing for Noah.

We were hopeful to be able to share with everyone the exciting news of our pregnancy after that meeting, but instead, we were sent for testing and specialist appointments. I was walking out to our truck to put Walker in his carseat while Hannah sat and cried with the sonographer on a bench, waiting for blood to be drawn. Normally, I would let Walker hold my hand and walk through the parking lot, but not this afternoon. The shadow of death had fallen over our family, and I couldn't help but snatch him up and carry him in my weary arms. Would I ever be able to let him go? How would I explain this to him? As I opened the door to my truck, the tears started to flow. It was all I could do to get Walker strapped into the carseat.

Our parents and several dear friends knew that we had a doctor's appointment. How were we supposed to update them? How was I supposed to communicate the horrors of what we had just heard? As a young husband and father, how was I going to lead our family? How were we ever going to get through this?

I climbed into my seat, cranked my truck to give Walker some AC, and collapsed onto the steering wheel. I hit my head against the steering wheel as my body convulsed in tears and agony, replaying that piercing word: abnormalities. I had never felt the depth from which this pain was coming. My groaning and weeping were coming from a part of me that I didn't even know existed. I can be an emotional person, but something inside of me had broken open that honestly frightened me. If I could hurt this badly this early during our pregnancy, what would it feel like if we had the chance to see pictures of his little face on the sonogram, or actually got to hold and kiss him? Hannah and I were just wading out into the murky waters of grief, not knowing the depth or how long we would be able to hold our heads above water.

One of the mistakes we made early on was being the ones to update everyone. That first evening and the next day, we undertook the exhausting task of about 15 calls, updating friends and family in between reading every article I could find about Trisomy 13. Each phone call was a crushing blow as we shared that we were okay, but hurting, and with a lot to process. And that we believed God would heal our son, on this side of eternity or the next. There was an audible gasp on the other end of the phone, and tears were flowing on both sides of the phone call.

Friends and family wept on the other side of the phone as we shared the devastating diagnosis. Tears of pain and confusion. So much pain, so much confusion, so many prayers. These people were asking meaningful questions that were so difficult to answer in the moment. Their love for our family was evident in their heartbreak for us, but I can remember telling Hannah towards the end of the next day, I can't keep doing this. I have to relive it each time we tell someone. Rob and Deandra brought us dinner that next evening, and provided the first of many wise counselling sessions.

They were willing to be the point person to communicate updates out, so that we only had to provide updates once. This was truly a godsend. The more intense the grief, the longer the time needed to process. Having to share updates with friends and family over and over again, prevented us from processing. I imagine this experience as if I had just slammed my hand in a car door. In the moments afterwards, my goal is not to slam my hand again in the door or to knock it on anything. I need to hold it close to me, trying not to say all of the words that come to mind, and allow my heart rate to normalize as I assess if my hand is broken or not. By continuing to share new updates time after time on the phone, it was as if I kept putting my hand by the door to be closed over and over, never allowing myself time to hold the hurting limb and breathe.

The rhythm that we found was to update our parents and the Baileys (Rob and Deandra), then we would take time to process. Sometimes this took hours, sometimes days. And then I would write. I would write an update of our family, and Hannah would read over it to make comments as needed. Then we would post it and send it to those not on social media. This rhythm was sustainable for us. Grief is not a sprint; it's a grueling ultramarathon. Pacing would become essential for our young family in the days, months, and years to come.

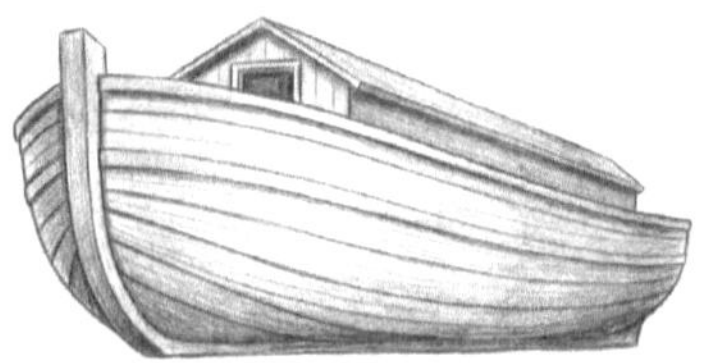

THE ARK: Find someone to be the communication manager for your family.

If you have recently entered a season of grief, I cannot recommend enough creating a rhythm of communication for your family. You will have many good-intentioned people around you wanting updates, but in this moment, you don't have to be strong for them. Tell someone because speaking your emotions out loud is a valuable resource in attempting to process them. Then, let your confidant share updates with others around you. You can also use social media, blogs, or other platforms to share how others can stay updated on your journey and engage with you in prayer, but don't get caught up in responding to every comment. You will not be able to be available to everyone. It's easy to fool yourself into allocating precious emotional energy to well-intentioned people. Preserve that energy for yourself and your immediate family.

For our family, those first few days were a blur. We did all that we could to not worry and to stay busy. I told our staff what was happening and that I would be taking several days off. Thankfully, they had been empowered to work on their day-to-day tasks without me there to micromanage every aspect of their tasks. Anything that needed my attention was emailed to me, and a few times a week, I checked my email. Outside of that, our phones were off; we needed space and time, and then we needed to see our family.

During this timeframe, I started journaling. Below is an excerpt from those days of waiting without answers.

It has been a painful, almost surreal eleven days. We talked about the potential implications of what was shared with us by our doctor, but we tried to reassure ourselves that it was not worth our worry until we knew more of what was actually happening. We know that this didn't surprise God, but it blindsided us. Minutes turned to hours, which turned to days. Waiting. And waiting. If you know me, you know I don't wait very well. We spent the weekend with family, and many people were praying for us. We tried to be around people, but couldn't bring ourselves to get out. We believed and told many people that God would heal Noah, this side of eternity or the next. We were reminded of Job's example that Even If Noah isn't healed on this side of eternity, We Will still praise God. Even If, We Will.

We wanted to be excited when we read the ultrasound results that we were having another boy, but it wouldn't come. We cried, we prayed, we sat in silence. We read, we sang, and we cried some more. We were told to wait until we heard from our test results before googling and stressing. We believe that life begins at conception, so we chose to name our sweet boy, Noah Clifton Efird. Noah means to rest, or rest in God, and Clifton is after my Papaw, who was a valiant man of God. We knew that his name would be fitting because it was the only place we could find rest in this turmoil, and our prayer was that even in the midst of our suffering, God would be glorified.

Rest while waiting is nearly impossible; from 9/17/19 on, we were constantly waiting.

We were emotionally drained by the time we got the call to discuss our test results on Monday, September 23rd. When your doctor asks if you want to come into the office to go over your results, you know they normally aren't good. Instead of waiting another day, we chose to receive the news. On this call, our kind doctor shared that our genetic testing had come back with elevated levels of Chromosome 13. Trisomy 13. This explained all of the abnormalities that were shown on our ultrasound. Several terms were said that I still don't know the meaning of. Heavy, loaded, definitive, mind-numbing statistics were shared. We stood in shock. We asked a couple of questions and then got off the phone. When heartache hits, you don't really know how you will respond. We just stood in a blur of confusion. I prayed over our family: Even If, We Will.

We were hopeful for clarity and prayerful for good news to come in our meeting with the specialist, some 48 hours later. Maybe we would be part of the less than 1%. Maybe it would be a false positive. Or maybe if it was a true positive and our ultrasound was not detailed enough yet, maybe it was translocational or mosaic trisomy 13, diagnoses that more often support life outside of the womb. We were hurting but hopeful, lost, and once again waiting: facing more tears, more pain, and more confusion.

Our specialist appointment was long and devastating. While the staff was caring and compassionate, the information they were sharing was downright that of nightmares. Not only was the diagnosis Trisomy 13, but it was also advanced. The blueprint that his body was being built from was off. As of Wednesday, September 25th, he was growing at an appropriate rate, but there were more abnormalities: heart defects and holes, kidney issues, and concerns with his neck and face. From what the doctors could see of his tiny body, there was no positive outlook. It was more difficult than I thought it would be to see him on the ultrasound screen. To see him move. To see his face, his arms, and his legs. To imagine the fun we were having with Walker growing up, and not seeing Noah there with our family on this journey we call life.

Anytime you put a face with a name, it somehow makes them feel more real. Our sweet boy had a name and a face. Our Noah was growing but had been given a lethal diagnosis. We were expected to carry him to term, but we didn't know enough about how long or if at all he would survive outside of the womb. At that time, it didn't look like long, but we didn't know enough yet. A normal pregnancy from the outside, but internally filled with pain. *Even If* became *Even Though*. Not the loss of hope, but the refining of it. Even Though the diagnosis is fatal, We Will praise God. *Even Though, We Will*. Our prayers of healing continued, but we added something. We prayed that God would prepare our hearts for what lay ahead of us.

Soon after our first specialist appointment, I wrote the following in my journal:

One day, when we move from hurting to healing, we too will walk this journey with families who are hurting. This is not a part of our family's testimony that we desired, but it will be part of our story nonetheless. Even Though, We Will. We are okay but hurting. We are not perfect, and we will not be perfect through this journey. We appreciate your prayers and your concerns. At this time, we truly don't know what we need, but we do know that we don't want special treatment or to be pitied. You are welcome to call or text; just don't be alarmed or take offense if or when we don't respond. When you see us out and about, there is no need to avoid us or not ask how we are doing. Just know, we will go through periods of wanting to talk and periods of not wanting to update everyone. We will provide updates as we have them and choose to share them. And we will reach out when we know what else we need. Feel free to share our updates with anyone wanting to journey with us. We still believe that God will heal our sweet Noah, and we are praying for a miracle. We ask that you pray with us and for us. Pray for patience with each other, as this is the most difficult thing our family has ever been through. Pray for rest. Pray for the medical staff and counselors that we work alongside. Pray for peace. Pray for our extended family and friends as they hurt and grieve alongside us. We have a long road ahead of us, with many lows and highs. Even Though, We Will.

Looking back, that message became a quiet guide for how we would survive the months ahead. We were riding the waves of emotion, and we had a lot left to process. We longed to mirror

David's example that we see in 2 Samuel 12:22-23 of praying, fasting, crying, and longing for healing for our sweet son. We sought to find times to worship in the waiting. We found time for joy in the suffering. And when he was healed, we prayed that we would rise, bathe, and worship, because God is still good. We had medical professionals and families that had been through this journey walking alongside us.

I will always remember the day that I felt Noah moving. Smiles and tears. Pride and sorrow. My sweet son was strong enough that I could feel him at 17 weeks, a full month before Walker. We thought feeling him move would only be painful, but in God's mercy, we were able to see some joy. We often reminded ourselves that Noah means to rest or rest in God, a truth that our family clung to in the midst of our storm.

We were riding the waves of emotions as a family. We allowed ourselves to engage with the pain. Emotions within themselves are healthy; it's what we choose to do with them that can cause problems or create freedom and redemption. We were over-whelmed by the outpouring of love and prayers that flooded our sweet family. It was truly amazing, humbling, and awe-in-spiring. Every card, text, letter, message, and voicemail was read, listened to, and appreciated.

To the person reading this, hoping for insight into the suffering of a loved one, please know, you don't have to know the words to say. Neither do they. Neither did Hannah nor I. Every card, gift basket, dinner, and prayer is received with grateful, weary hearts.

Most days were a day filled with so many emotions. Each doctor appointment provided hope that our son was still growing, but realization of the diagnosis that awaited all of us. A path of grief for a loss we had not yet fully experienced. He was progressing and fighting. Yet more abnormalities still presented and validated that the blueprint was off. Trisomy 13 wreaked havoc on our sweet son's body. We looked at his precious image with thankful, heavy hearts that he was growing, but knowing what was yet to come.

I vividly remember the first time Walker said Noah's name. I'm sure it didn't sound like Noah to anyone else, but it was Noah. In a moment, we learned that joy and sorrow can share the same breath. We were filled with joy to see Walker excited about being a big brother while simultaneously overcome with sorrow for the absence that would become our family's reality. In God's mercy, our sweet firstborn Walker was coming to life and rapidly developing before our eyes. Throughout the process, he gave so much joy in the midst of pain. He still has the sweetest smile and most incredible compassion for Hannah and me. We chose to celebrate his growth rather than pity the disappearing images of Noah experiencing those same developmental steps.

The outcome seemed defined, but the way that we engaged with this journey was rooted in our perspective. We were assured of God's healing capacity and the power of prayer. We were confident that our sweet Noah would be healed, this side of eternity or the next. We were praying for a miracle, knowing that God was who He says He is. We knew, at the end of the day, He was God, and we were not, and we humbly submitted to Him. We rested in the assurance that we served an unchanging, merciful God: a God full of hope, working a plan for our good, for each member in our family. We were choosing hope. Even Though, We Will.

We chose to celebrate Noah's life, remembering each day for the blessing that it was. We found ways to celebrate his life while he was here and while we wait to see him again. We were on the journey from hurting to healing. We had many waves left to ride, but we knew that there would be redemption for Noah's life. This was not the story that our family wanted, but it was the story that we had been given. We were comforted that in the midst of our trial, we were not abandoned. We are hopeful to see this side of eternity, the impact of sweet Noah's life, and the opportunities it affords our family for the glory of God. We were held so close, embraced so tenderly by a sovereign God who is for us and who loves us. We were not overcome. We were finding the strength to stand. Even Though, We Will.

As we continued in our journey, my urge to write became stronger and stronger. It provided me with a way to articulate the feelings in my soul. It also allowed me a way to encourage and challenge others who were following our journey. I didn't update as much as I had hoped to, because each post took so much out of me. While an avenue to process, it was an exhausting experience.

I remember a song that I was introduced to by an old friend, Andrew Brown, called Beautiful Exhaustion. In it, he describes the weight of Jesus' example and how we are called to live like it. He reminds us of the calling to lay all that we have at the feet of Jesus, which can lead to this place of outward exhaustion but inward satisfaction as we seek to find solace in the Maker of Heaven and Earth. I felt that calling as I wrote those updates during the pregnancy and in the months after Noah went to be with Jesus. I felt this intense calling to share in our grief, which can be described as a beautiful exhaustion. I'm not sure if he will pick up this book. However, Andrew, thank you for listening to God all those years ago when you penned the words to this song. I come back to them often.

One moment that seemed pivotal was New Year's Eve, 2019. It felt as if we had been fighting this war of grief, but had not yet reached the front lines. Once we crested the hill into 2020, we knew what waited for us just months down the road. Little did we know that a global pandemic would be hitting as well.

Here is the journal entry that I made on New Year's Eve.

Triumph and tragedy. These words stand out as we look back over this year. 2019 has been a rewarding, challenging, depressing, and quiet year. From celebrating Walker's first birthday office style to achieving and surpassing many business and family goals to celebrating our fifth anniversary by doing one of our favorite things (traveling to a new city), this year has provided many joyous things to celebrate. New friends who treat us as family. New challenges we overcame as a family. A new depth to our relationship as a couple and as a young family that has felt called to expand. A richer understanding of the application of the I Am statements from our family mission:

As an Efird,
I am redeemed by God.
I am unconditionally loved.
I am joyfully content.
I am abiding in grace.
I am seeking justice.
I am loving mercy.
I am walking humbly with God.
A new mantra serving as the heartbeat for our family:
Even Though, We Will

For years, these statements had served as a family mission, but on September 17, they stopped being words on a page and started being the building blocks for our Ark. 'Joyfully content' didn't mean we were happy about a terminal diagnosis; it meant we were anchored in a peace that surpassed all understanding. 'Loving mercy' became a daily requirement when we were too tired to be kind to one another. Our identity hadn't changed, but the weight of it certainly had.

We sit here on this last day of 2019 with tears as we thank God for the many triumphs in 2019, yet with our triumphs has come one of the most deafening tragedies we could never imagine.

In the midst of tragedy, it is often hard to find triumph. In the waves of emotion that cascade over you unexpectedly, unpredictably, and inconveniently, triumph can feel forced and often faked. September 17th, 2019, was a day we never saw coming, with a diagnosis that we have struggled to digest in the 105 days since. A new appreciation for community, family, friends, coworkers, Good Samaritans, and our faith in Jesus Christ. A deeper understanding of grief and empathy. A fresh perspective on taking life one day at a time. Anguished, helpless, exhausted, hurting but never hopeless. Even Though, We Will

From text messages and care packages to t-shirts, cards, books, dinners, hand-knit prayer shawls, and prayers, we have been overwhelmed by the outpouring of love over the last few months. So many people have been praying for our little family and our precious Noah, and we covet your prayers. There has been a sweet tenderness to God's mercy in allowing us to feel your thoughts and prayers, and we are forever grateful for the strength they have provided each of us. At this time, we know that Noah's kidneys are grossly enlarged, which could lead to renal failure and being unable to carry him to term. We are living with this reality each week as we seek to celebrate each day and find joy in the midst of our grief. We know that Noah's cerebellum is starting to fall behind on development, as well as showing additional abnormalities. We also know that his heart has a large hole and missing connections between arteries, both of which will not support life outside of the womb for more than a few minutes. Our current reality shows that we will not have much time, if any, with our precious son. We continue to pray with a confident expectation, the following: Lord, we pray that you will heal baby Noah and prepare our hearts for what is to come. We would ask that you join us in praying this over our family. We have many difficult, crushing decisions to make over the coming weeks as we enter the 3rd trimester. We have been through the difficulty of pregnancy before, but we are wrestling with what the first contraction with Noah means for our family. We ask that you pray Psalm 23 over us.

Psalm 23:4-6: "Yea, though I walk through the valley of the shadow of death, I will fear no evil; For You are with me; Your rod and Your staff, they comfort me. You prepare a table before me in the presence of my enemies; You anoint my head with oil; My cup runs over. Surely goodness and mercy shall follow me. All the days of my life; And I will dwell in the house of the Lord. Forever."

As a family, we are longing to find purpose for our pain. We are fighting to see through our valley as the shadow of death looms over us, each day bringing it closer. We are intent on feeling His rod and His staff as they protect and provide for us. And in the midst of this shadow, we know that we have been prepared an incredible table. Not a seat meant just for our family, but a table that is being expanded for others to come, sit, and see the Goodness and Mercy of God. This is not the story nor the table that our family wanted, but it is the story and table that we have been given. We ask for your prayers as we seek ways to pull up additional seats at our table. Even Though, We Will

The holidays brought many emotions. We are finding different hurdles throughout our tragedy that seem to be part of dealing with grief: Hurting, Healing, and Helping. We are seeking to engage with each hurdle, process the emotions that come with each, and move through them as His Rod and His Staff lead us. This is not a process we can hurry, yet we find ourselves moving through each hurdle depending on the day. We are so thankful for the grace we have received from so many of you in accepting whatever hurdle we find ourselves in that day.

2020 is the start of a new year and a new decade. We have a lot on our horizon for this upcoming year and upcoming decade, many of which we can't see or imagine. What we can see is raw and painful, yet peaceful, knowing that one day we will see our sweet Noah again. We will continue to find time to fast and pray and to rise, bathe, and worship. A sincere thank you to all of you who are supporting us along this journey. We may not yet have the strength to thank you personally, but please know that you are not being missed by our family. Likewise, we encourage you to find room at your own table. There is something healing found in generosity. Allow God to redeem your story so someone else can embrace His Goodness and Mercy. Even Though, We Will

The holidays were hard. To say it was difficult to go see family and friends would be an understatement. Traditions felt bland, and conversations heavy. Walker was blossoming into this incredibly tender and outgoing little boy, and we found great joy in the blessing of his life, all the while struggling with the weight of Noah's. Hannah and I intentionally went to events like concerts and plays, knowing that it would be the only time we could let Noah experience them.

The first day of the new year and new decade did not bring excitement. I am one who loves new things. I enjoy change and variation, but I couldn't get excited about the new that was directly in front of us. We had this goal to make it through the holidays before we made any arrangements with the hospital or for the memorial service. Now, we had to face a new reality: palliative care team meetings at the local hospitals to discuss our plan for end-of-life care for our precious Noah. We had to call the funeral home and utter the words, "I need to talk with someone about burial arrangements for my son, who will be born in a few months." 2020 had arrived along with the third trimester, and we were dragged back out into the seas again.

One of the decisions we had to make was where Noah would be delivered. This delivery would look much different than Walker's delivery. Our OBGYN practice set up meetings with the palliative care team at the local hospitals. These palliative care teams were filled with amazing individuals who have answered the call to serve grieving parents such as Hannah and me, as they talk you through the process for end-of-life care for your child. Both teams were very kind, but we felt an instant connection with one over the other. We submitted all of our registration information and walked through their parent survey.

We tried to use each platform as an opportunity to share hope and prayers for the people we were coming into contact with. While we were experiencing this season on a very personal level, these professionals walk through it with families like ours every single day. We couldn't help but share encouragement and prayers with them. Each time, our encouragement was met with a heartfelt thank you as tears were held back. So much sacrifice, with very little appreciation. These people were helping us navigate life with Noah, so we wanted to do all that we could to thank them. They had seen this story play out for families before, with varying results.

As we were leaving the palliative care meeting, our doctor wisely pulled me aside. He asked if we had a strong marriage. I responded that I had been very blessed to marry a wonderful woman and that we strived to love each other very well. He said, "good because the next year of your life will always go one of two ways. It will either drive you together, or it will drive a wedge between you. I've seen it sneak up on couples too many times. Take the time to be together as a couple and allow this to draw you closer." I am so thankful for this pointed advice, as we only briefly felt the wedge that could have been driven between us.

THE ARK: Hope is not pretending the diagnosis isn't real; it is trusting God even when it is.

CHAPTER 4

HOARDING TIME

Stealing sacred moments from death.

As I write this, I'm lying in a stiff, uncomfortable chair-bed in the hospital, snuggling my precious son and thanking God for the time we continue to have with him. The birth went incredibly fast. Hannah woke up about 3 a.m. feeling contractions. Little did we know that 4 hours later, we'd be meeting our Noah. On the way to the hospital, I struggled to fight through the tears. Hannah's pain escalated so quickly that I was afraid we wouldn't make it to the hospital. He came quickly. We started checking into the hospital at 6:55 a.m., and we were holding him by 7:40 a.m. At first, he wasn't breathing. He didn't have much color. We thought he had passed during labor.

Then his precious cry broke through.

His lungs were underdeveloped, and we could hear him fighting to remove the fluid. Then his color began to come, and he started looking around. We placed him skin-to-skin with Hannah, cherishing every moment. Tears flowed from my eyes. This son of mine, whom I had prayed for, wept for, and hurt for, was finally here. And he was fighting to breathe, fighting to see. As the medical team cared for Hannah, I had the honor of swaddling him and holding him. Wave after wave of emotion washed over me.

I prayed for him. I thanked God for a live birth and for the opportunity to see our son, to hear him cry, and to hold him as he breathed. I prayed that God would take him from my arms into His arms whenever it was time. We prayed over him for healing, generational impact, holy redemption, and peace. We talked to him about his big brother, Walker. About the helipad visible from our hospital window. We cherished every moment, grateful for the gift of time with him. Noah met his brother, his grandparents, his uncle, his pastor, his friends, and his doctor and nursing staff. So many smiles. So many tears. So many thankful hearts for the time we had with Noah.

From very early on, we knew that time would be much briefer than normal. We had prepared ourselves for no time to a couple of hours. We prayed for time, but had no clue what was to come. Seconds turned to minutes. Minutes to hours. Before we knew it, we were eating dinner with friends in our room, discussing our plan for the night. We had prepared for many situations, but honestly, not this one. The information surrounding the condition of his heart, lungs, kidneys, and brain didn't leave much room for extended periods of time. So much gratitude.

We learned that Noah snored (like many Efird men before him). Also, his feet were very ticklish, like his brother and dad. Tender, sweet moments offered from a loving Heavenly Father. We were blessed to see him smile, yawn, cry, hiccup, fart, sleep, snuggle, and eat. Each moment was a sweet blessing.

Because the delivery was so quick, the nursing staff grabbed our phones to take pictures and videos. Everyone was prepared for the delicacy of time with Noah, and each honored it with such care and professionalism. They congratulated us and sang Hannah's praises (if she needed another check mark for Wonder Woman, a fully natural birth certainly earned it). A dear friend who is a professional photographer arrived in time to take pictures, but this was no normal delivery.

We are deeply thankful for the pictures taken by both the staff and our professional photographer, and we will cherish them for the rest of our lives. It took a few years for us to look at them, but I'm so thankful we have them. Some are set as backgrounds or displayed on a digital picture frame; others are stored away for a later day. We chose to share several of them in this book because we cherish the memories and the story they tell.

You can see some of our favorites on the following pages.

Noah

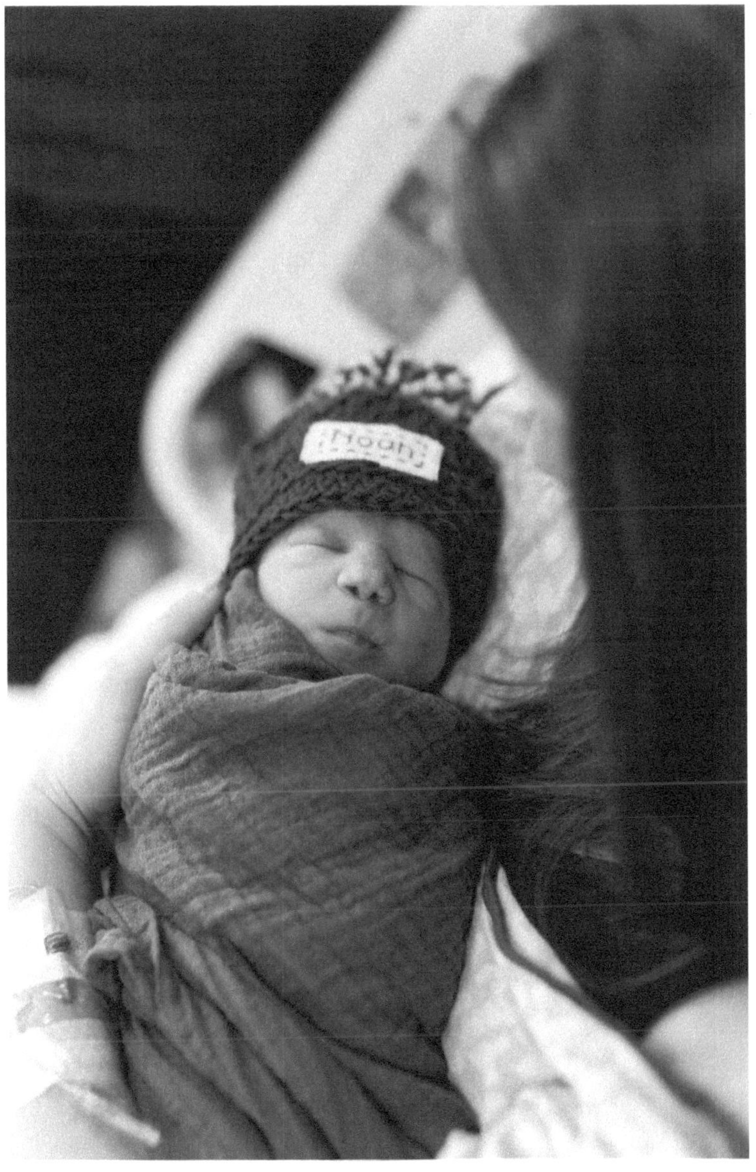

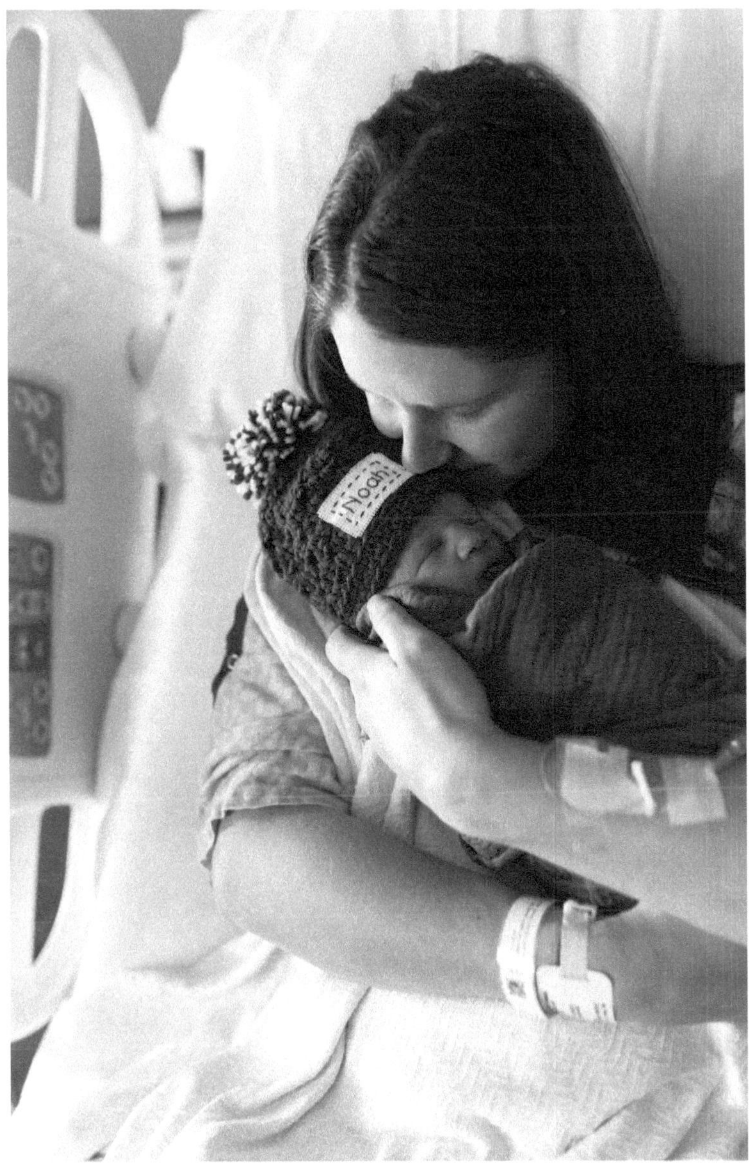
Noah!

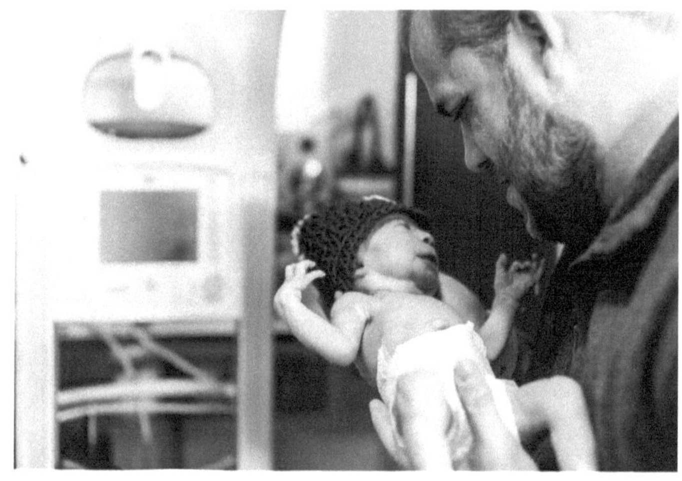

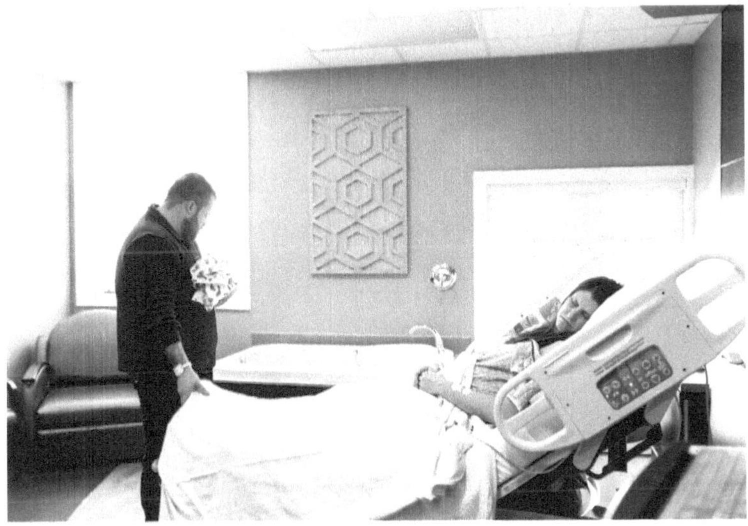

We believe the birth was so fast because a delayed delivery might have placed too much stress on Noah's body. We believe the speed at which he came into this world allowed us more time with him on this side of eternity. Part of the rawness of this moment for us, and specifically Hannah, is the amount of pain and sacrifice during pregnancy and childbirth to not reap what most parents expect as the reward. When they handed Walker to Hannah, she looked at me and said, "*It was totally worth it!*" The simple fact that she chose a second journey into pregnancy was validation enough. We believe that all life begins at conception and should be cherished. Still, the pregnancy and birth carried a looming reality: the amount of sacrifice and pain our young family would endure, knowing it would be cut painfully short of the reward we had hoped for. But that's what love does: it sacrifices. Love is sacrifice; it is the giving of yourself for someone else.

I watched in amazement as my bride gave of herself throughout the pregnancy, fought through a fast delivery, and then tenderly cherished the hours we had with Noah, as only a redeemed mother could. A mother redeemed by the love of Jesus Christ is a force to be reckoned with. As parents, we are best equipped to love our children from a place of redemption in God's love for us, both individually and as a couple. It would have been easier to guard our hearts by letting Noah go before he was born, or even immediately afterward. We chose to sacrifice our hearts in honoring his life. We chose to love.

We chose to mirror the love of our Savior, who died on a cross, knowing that many He died for would never return that love. The reward of that relationship would be but a passing vapor in the midst of eternity. But God, who is rich in mercy, gave Himself for our sins so that you and I might be in a relationship with Him. Hannah and I tried our very best to be rooted in this love. This love that sacrifices no matter the return. In God's infinite mercy and grace, we were met with such tender moments. Our sacrifice, while costly, was well worth the investment. It was almost as if time slowed down during the hours that we were able to spend with Noah.

The first night, we refused to sleep. The three of us cuddled together, in awe of the time we had. Our nurses came in regularly to check on Noah, and his breathing and heart rate held steady. For the first time in this journey, we were both overwhelmed with gratitude. You never expect to have to prepare yourself to say goodbye to your children, yet we had been preparing ourselves for nearly seven months. Some of us expected not to spend the night in the hospital. Thankfully, we had packed a change of clothes and items to shower with, but every additional breath felt as though we were stealing moments from death.

We hugged, snuggled, kissed, and loved him fiercely. We would stand in the midst of the valley of the shadow of death for as long as we could. Thankfully, friends and the hospital staff brought us food. Bathroom breaks were brief, not wanting to waste a moment away from him. We took turns holding him, never knowing if handing him over would be the last time we held him alive. Every kiss was tender. Every word was intentional. Every emotion was on high alert. After that first night, we were physically and emotionally exhausted, yet spiritually full. In conversations with our doctors and friends afterward, there was a deep sense of peace and gratitude in our hearts. Even in exhaustion, we were held by peace.

Our day-shift nurse was pleasantly surprised to see us still there the next morning. She shared stories of her family and helped us get footprints and mementos of our sweet Noah. Every one of our nurses showed remarkable compassion. Once we passed the 24-hour mark, we could begin to see the signs of Noah's lethal diagnosis visually. We could see that his kidneys were failing and that his heart was struggling to pump blood through his body. Aside from the brief moments when our photographer took pictures of him in his hospital crib, he was held every second of every hour, and he would be held until he passed from this side of eternity to the next.

By day two, more friends had stopped by the hospital. After we passed the 24-hour mark, we had a run-in with a young nurse practitioner who did not handle our situation with much bedside manner. Thankfully, our nurse and our pastor went to bat for us, and we were able to meet with someone from the NICU team. It was a very painful reminder of the power of words and the importance of listening before speaking. That Sunday, Noah received a full examination from the on-site neonatologist, and he confirmed the uncertainty of Noah's condition. Sometimes Trisomy 13 babies will live for days, weeks, months, or years.

We were thrown back into the waves as he began discussing the possibility of going home with hospice care. I remember everyone leaving the room. Hannah and I held Noah and just cried. We looked at each other and asked the looming question: *What are we going to do?* We were also told that Noah would need to be moved into the NICU so we could receive more specialized care. Prior to delivery, we had met with both the NICU and the palliative care team. We felt very confident in both of their abilities to care for our family, but we never expected to actually need the NICU team. Our sweet Noah was a fighter, and it felt as though he was responding to the weight of our sacrifice by hanging on a little while longer.

Late on day two, they moved us to a private room in the NICU. No one knew how long we would have with Noah, but the staff wanted to make sure that we had privacy and the space to cherish every moment. I remember walking through the dimly lit NICU, curtains drawn, families throughout the room sitting with children fighting for life. Heart monitors and oxygen sensors were beeping. We were entering a war zone where many families before us had fought with their presence and prayers for their children. As we stepped into the apartment-style room toward the back, I didn't yet know this would be the only home Noah would know in this life. It had a full bed, a rocking chair, instruments and tubing lining the walls, and a small desk in the corner. Without the medical equipment, it felt much like a college apartment.

The room felt like a coordinated battle between life and death. The cold, rhythmic beeping of monitors and the sterile smell of hospital soap fought against the warm, sweet scent of Noah's skin and the soft weight of his body in my arms. Every time a monitor chirped, it was a reminder that death was in the room, but every time he hiccuped, it was a reminder that life was winning, for now. We weren't just passing time; we were hoarding it.

We set our things down, held each other, and cried. We each kissed Noah, and we prayed. We prayed for wisdom and discernment; for peace and patience; for God's mercy in a clear path as we discussed what our next steps would be.

Before we could get far into the conversation, Noah had his first gasping episode. The image and sound of his gasp are burned deeply into me. We frantically searched for the phone and called the desk. By the time our nurse rushed in, Noah was breathing again and looking as normal as he could at this point in his journey. She checked his vitals and updated the doctor, who then came in to update us. Noah's heart was starting to shut down, and he had made the decision for us about whether hospice care was needed. I can remember the warmth of the tears as they streamed down my face on well-worn paths. We had just prayed for God's mercy on our young family, and He was answering that prayer. Many of the doctors throughout our journey assured us that Noah would not be in pain and that the most loving thing we could do was to love him well while he was here. To hold him, to kiss him, and to tell him about the world outside of the hospital. We did exactly that all through the second night as well. But this night was far more difficult.

Night two was a battle for us. We had entered an emotional and spiritual war zone. As we approached being awake for forty-eight hours, our bodies began forcing us to sleep, so alternating short naps became the best solution we could manage. We took turns sleeping at 15-20 minute intervals while the other held Noah. Worship music streamed constantly from our phones. Soft prayers were whispered over him as we slowly rocked him. Each time I closed my eyes, I didn't know if it would be the last time I saw him alive. We never wanted Noah to be alone, and for his entire life, he wasn't. This truth was a cherished thought in the midst of such grief.

His gasping episodes continued throughout the night into the morning. Each time, our nurses graciously came in to check on him and on us. The final twelve hours were the hardest. It was a slow fade we were not prepared for. Death is a cruel reality, caused by the presence of sin in our world. We were coming face-to-face with this brutal truth. The primary neonatologist we had met with had been out of town with his family when we arrived at the hospital. He had arrived late Monday afternoon, and he stopped in to see us. He is one of the main reasons that we chose their hospital for care, so we were thankful for the opportunity for him and Noah to meet. We were describing Noah's episodes as the doctor was preparing to look over his charts and information that our specialist sent when Noah had his final episode.

Noah passed in my arms. He went from earthly father to Heavenly Father (I later learned this was a tender prayer from my gracious wife. She had carried him for so long that she wanted me to be the one holding him in his final moments on earth.)

As I wept, I couldn't look up. I couldn't move. I couldn't breathe. I held him close and wept. I rocked in the green rocking chair listening to worship music, holding this tiny son of mine. My sweet, strong boy was now with Jesus. We had fervently prayed for God to heal our son, and in that crushing moment, He had answered that prayer. He was completely healed from Trisomy 13 and was in the presence of our Heavenly Father. I knew that he wouldn't return to us, but that we would go to him. Yes, this provided hope, but it did not remove the crushing ache within my soul.

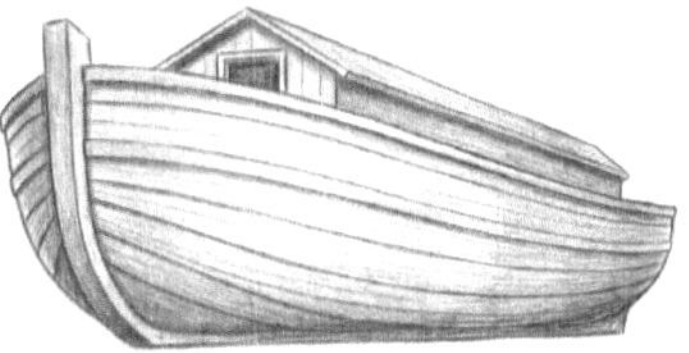

THE ARK: When nothing can be done, presence becomes the greatest expression of love.

THE MOMENTS AFTER

The Chair and the Cart: Trading an inward grief for a sacred compassion.

Everyone exited the room, giving our young family privacy in this devastating moment. Hannah and I each took time to hold him and etch every inch of his face into our memories. In a moment, he went from our presence to the presence of our Savior. What remained was his earthly body, ravaged by disease. All the more, we held him with the tenderness you would offer any baby. We knew he wasn't there anymore, and we still held on. Looking back, neither of us remembers how long we stayed in these moments. His face was stained with our tears and our drawn-out kisses. This son of ours was gone. There were no words to share with each other; only looks of devastation. We held each other and wept. The moment we had been preparing for over months had crashed over us. In a moment, we went from parents grieving a sick child to parents grieving the death of a child. We didn't realize how impactful this distinction would be. We knew where he had gone; now we had to figure out where we were to go.

The nurse eventually broke the silence, letting us know they would need to take Noah to prepare him for the funeral home. Handing over my son was the hardest thing I've ever done. The weight was crushing. Hannah and I embraced in tears. There were no words to share. What had been wailing softened into quiet sobs as we held each other. Nothing prepares you for this moment. The moment you've known was coming. The moment the outcome of the diagnosis is final, and nothing more can be done. The moment you realize that you won't be able to see your child again on this side of heaven. The moment hung like a thick fog in the room. It felt as though my heart had been torn in two. I experienced the pain of saying goodbye to my son while watching my best friend do the same.

I wasn't prepared for seeing Hannah go through grief. She has an infectious smile and a warmth that lights up a room. There is a light behind her eyes that draws you in during conversation, and an empathy in the way she listens and connects with whomever she's speaking with. In this moment, I saw her as she had seen me, completely broken. The warmth, the light, the tenderness had left her in this moment. We stood alongside each other, fully broken yet not fully hopeless.

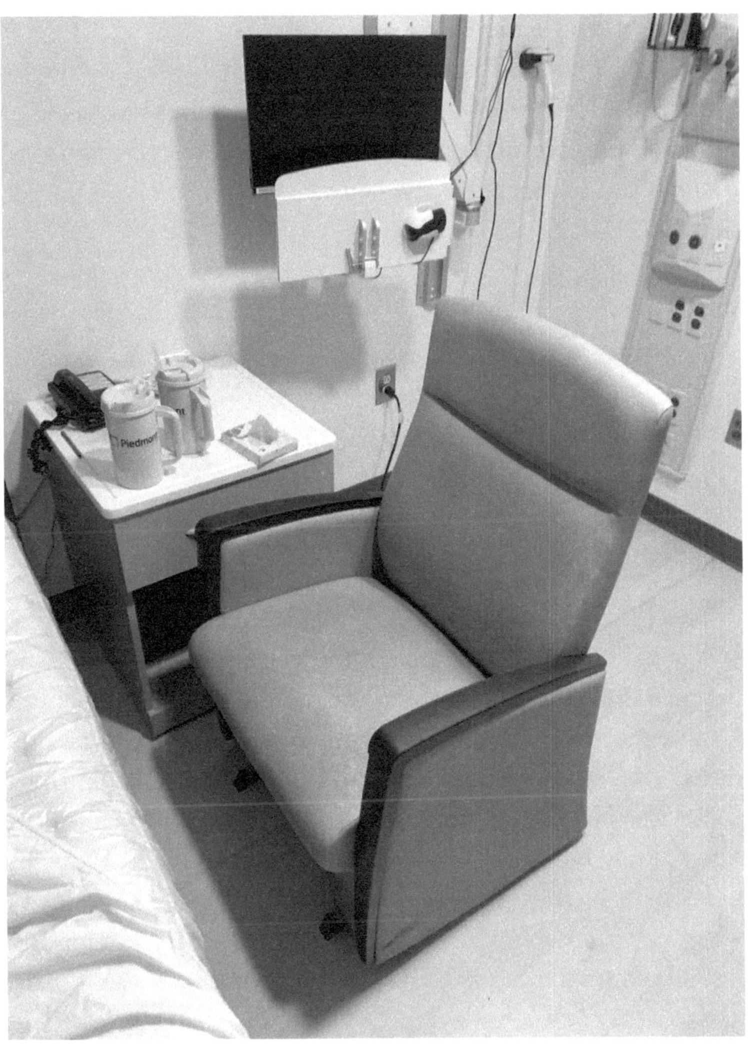

The nurse returned with some of the clothing items that we wanted to keep as mementos of Noah's life. We gathered our few belongings. We embraced once more, taking in the room, and then we left. Right before I stepped out the door, I snapped this picture of the rocking chair. That chair forever changed me. That chair held me as I held my son. That chair is where my son passed from this side of eternity into the next. That chair is where I fully experienced my grief. That chair will forever remind me that God can answer our prayers in ways we do not see fit. That chair reminds me that it's okay to not be okay. That chair reminds me that when our troubles do not feel light and momentary, I must fix my eyes on what is unseen.

> *"Therefore, we do not lose heart. Though outwardly we are wasting away, yet inwardly we are being renewed day by day. For our light and momentary troubles are achieving for us an eternal glory that far outweighs them all. So we fix our eyes not on what is seen, but on what is unseen, since what is seen is temporary, but what is unseen is eternal."*
>
> *2 Corinthians 4:16-18 NIV*

It was here that I felt as though I had truly lost heart. I could only see the present. The future was far too cloudy and painful. I knew that I would one day see my son again, but in the moments as we walked out of the NICU room, all I could think about was putting one foot in front of the other. I pushed the cart holding our belongings with one hand and held Hannah's hand in the other. We rode the elevator down to the lobby, where my truck was parked. After getting Hannah and our stuff loaded, I took the cart back inside. It was in this moment that I learned a very valuable lesson.

The young woman working the front desk had no idea what the last several hours of my life had been like. I walked up to her with the cart and asked if I could leave it there so I didn't have to go back upstairs. She informed me that it was not her job and that I needed to return it. Maybe it was because of how emotionally drained I was, a prompting from the Holy Spirit, or a combination of the two, but instead of directing my frustration at this young lady in the moment, I silently shook my head. After the elevator dropped me back at the NICU floor, I pushed the cart back into the unit. As soon as the doors opened, I was hit with this realization. All of these families were waiting to make the walk we had just made. They were all praying to make it with their child, but the same path lay ahead of all of them.

My moment of individual grief had been so inwardly focused. How could *I* ever go forward? How could *I* ever find hope and joy in my life again? In this moment, I realized how much we were not alone. I realized how fragile all of our lives truly are. I walked past her again, but the woman who had just been an obstacle was now an image-bearer. I didn't see someone who was 'just doing her job'; I saw someone who, like everyone else in that lobby, was one ultrasound or one phone call away from the same dimly lit unit I had just left.

My grief hadn't been removed, but my heart had been widened. I was forever changed in that chair, but it took returning to that room to realize the change wasn't just about my loss, it was about our shared need for grace. I woke up the next day with a new set of eyes to see the world around me. Walking, talking, image bearers of God, struggling with our present reality, longing for a better tomorrow.

THE ARK: We find true redemption not by escaping our pain, but by allowing God to lead us back to the very place where our grief began.

We often think that happiness and joy are the same emotion, but while similar, their sources are polar opposites. Happiness is driven by external circumstances. It comes and goes as the stimulus comes and goes. We chase the feeling of happiness far too often. This pursuit of something fleeting is why so many in our culture are overweight, overworked, dependent on alcohol, or buried in debt. We feel the moment of happiness, but it eventually fades. There was nothing happy about the moment that we found ourselves in, but we couldn't help but sense the presence of joy in our lives. We certainly were not happy, but we sensed a grounding and a presence. Joy is formed internally, and our joy was not rooted in worldly things; it was rooted in God. We sensed God's presence in the midst of our suffering, and it gave us a tangible peace. His presence allowed space in our souls to hurt while also holding onto the truth of our future reunion with Noah. This sense came from maturing as a believer, and it redefined my definition of joy. Joy to me is the steady calming of my soul in the promises and the presence of my Savior.

"until we all reach unity in the faith and in the knowledge of the Son of God and become mature, attaining to the whole measure of the fullness of Christ. Then we will no longer be infants, tossed back and forth by the waves, and blown here and there by every wind of teaching and by the cunning and craftiness of people in their deceitful scheming. Instead, speaking the truth in love, we will grow to become in every respect the mature body of him who is the head, that is, Christ."

Ephesians 4:13-15 NIV

You and I understand that life is not a cakewalk. Trials will come, as many did for our family, but we were able to experience a deep well of joy flowing from an intimate relationship with Jesus Christ. A relationship that is also available to you. This relationship is the source of our joy in the midst of tragedy.

"But God demonstrates His own love toward us, in that while we were still sinners, Christ died for us."

Romans 5:8 NKJV

Jesus Christ died for you and me because His love led to sacrifice. The most generous and joyful thing He could have offered. Where our rebellion deserves death, His love gives life. He has offered to take your place. To give life where there was only death. To give hope where there was only hopelessness. We clung to this truth. We also knew the generational impact this could have. Our personal relationship with Jesus Christ became the banner our young family rallied underneath.

In the Old Testament, God used Moses to lead the children of Israel out of slavery in Egypt. Because of fear and hesitation in trusting the promises of God, they wandered in the wilderness for forty years. Joshua would then be the one to take them into the promised land. Toward the end of Joshua's life, after all the land had been divided up and the people settled into their inheritance, Joshua challenged the people to make a choice about whom they would serve: the gods of the world, or the one true God, YHWH. Joshua boldly declares a statement over his family, one you may recognize.

"But as for me and my house, we will serve the LORD."

Joshua 24:15 NKJV

Much like today, there were many things the people could worship and pursue. Joshua clearly defined the banner over his family.

When you move down to verse 31, you see the lasting impact of this declaration.

"Israel served the LORD all the days of Joshua, and all the days of the elders who outlived Joshua, who had known all the works of the LORD which He had done for Israel."

Joshua 24:31 NKJV

What banner will be placed over your family for the generations to come?

It's easy to feel abandoned by God in the midst of suffering, especially in death. From our earthly perspective, death feels final and leaves a lasting effect on those still living. We hurt. We miss deeply.

"But I do not want you to be ignorant, brethren, concerning those who have fallen asleep, lest you sorrow as others who have no hope. For if we believe that Jesus died and rose again, even so God will bring with Him those who sleep in Jesus."

1 Thessalonians 4:13–14 NKJV

Thank you, Jesus, for this hope.

"Jesus said to her, 'I am the resurrection and the life. He who believes in Me, though he may die, he shall live."

John 11:25 NKJV

Thank you, Jesus, for this assurance.

This is what held us when nothing else could.

THE ARK: Grief marks you permanently, but it does not mean God has abandoned you.

CHAPTER 6

HOLDING HIM UNTIL HEAVEN

From an earthly father's arms to the Heavenly Father's arms.

We left the hospital changed, but unsure how to live as changed people. The following words were written in the days and weeks after Noah passed. They were not written for a book, but for survival itself. They were written by a father trying to learn to breathe again. I've preserved them here with minimal editing, because they capture what grief sounded like before it learned to speak more quietly.

Noah Clifton Efird, our sweet, strong boy, was now with Jesus. Noah was born at 7:40 a.m. on March 7, 2020, and weighed 5lbs 5oz. We were able to celebrate as a family for 57.5 beautiful hours. He passed peacefully in my arms, a merciful answer to so many prayers, as he went from the loving, protective arms of his earthly father to the perfect, tender arms of his Heavenly Father. For so long, we had prayed for his healing, and at 5:15 p.m. on March 9, 2020, God graciously answered that prayer.

He snored like all Efird men. His feet were ticklish like his daddy's and older brother's. He had the sweetest coos and smile, and he was the best snuggler. We beamed with pride as we shared him with friends and family. We prayed fiercely over him: for redemption of his story, for celebration of his life, and for a generational impact of God's glory.

We are overwhelmed with gratitude for the tender time we were able to spend with him. Seconds turned to minutes, which turned to hours. Each hour was a precious gift. Unexpected time, received only with gratitude. We cried, we laughed, we loved, we worshiped, and we snuggled fiercely.

We were weeping and worshiping, seeking to grieve his passing and celebrate the time we had with him. We were deeply sad, yet eternally peaceful. Like his healing, God answered our prayers to prepare our family's hearts. Noah means rest, and we still sense God's presence as we rest in His faithfulness.

Here is a journal entry from the end of March, three weeks since we had held our precious Noah.

Goodbye.

Three weeks ago, we said Goodbye to our sweet boy. Not goodbye in the sense that he was lost or that we wouldn't see him again, but goodbye for a season. We knew where he was going and that he would not return to us, but that we would one day go to him. Goodbyes are never easy, but this one was gut-wrenching. Even when you know that you will be reunited with them, you still hurt in their absence. I will never forget letting the nurse take him out of our room. Overwhelming sorrow as our hearts wept, and the heaviness of our reality settled around us like a thick fog. As a father, I proudly shoulder the responsibility of protection and provision for my family. I am fiercely protective of my bride and my boys. In this moment, embracing my bride as we uncontrollably wept, I felt the weight of all of my inadequacies to truly protect and provide for my family. Neither physical strength, mental aptitude, emotional calming, nor financial prowess could stand under the weight of the pain of this goodbye. In the midst of the confusion, we prayed—no, cried out to God. We boldly proclaimed Even Though, We Will: that His ways are higher than our ways, that He will redeem Noah's story, that He will give comfort to the broken-hearted, that He will turn our mourning into dancing, that He will draw near, that we will see Noah again, and that He will remain the same today as He was yesterday as He will be tomorrow. Then we slowly packed our belongings, the nurse brought back the clothing items we had requested, and we walked out of the NICU. Nurses looked on, far too accustomed to this sight. We left the hospital as abruptly as we entered it. We were amazed at the 57.5 hours that we got to cuddle with our sweet boy, but we knew the road that lay ahead of us was far more difficult than we could ever imagine. We were deeply hurting but oddly peaceful, immensely grateful for the time we were blessed to know our son, to hold him, to pray over him, to sing to him, to share him with friends and family, and to tenderly love him. As we drove home, we talked about the sweet memories we had just created with our son, the only memories we would be able to create with him, fully knowing that the reality of missing him would soon hit. We delayed that reality as long as we could. Since then, we have both cried, laughed, danced, and sat in silence.

Grief comes in stages and looks different for everyone, but it becomes overwhelming when you try to carry all of it at once. We have learned to pray for grace for that day, some days praying to get to lunch and then praying at lunch to get to bed, and then in bed praying for the blessing of sleep, to wake up the next day and do it all over again.

"Therefore do not worry about tomorrow, for tomorrow will worry about its own things. Sufficient for the day is its own trouble." Matthew 6:34 NKJV

Focus dictates direction, so we are choosing to set our gaze on Jesus. Now more than ever, may we fix our eyes today on the One who is the Prince of Peace.

"Okay" feels like a shell of how we are actually feeling. Our family is together and healthy, but very raw, hurting, and healing. Death is a cruel finality, ultimately for the ones still living. We are thankful that Noah is healed and that God is continuing to prepare our hearts to walk on this side of Goodbye. We carry forward one day at a time, seeking to celebrate and honor the life of our sweet boy. We boldly proclaim God's glory and His anointing over Noah's story. We are finding rest in the midst of God's embrace. His goodness and mercy are pursuing us.

Looking back now, I can see how much of that writing was breathless, how grief demanded words simply to survive the day. I didn't yet know what healing would look like, only that God was near. These words mark the place where sorrow was loud, and faith was quiet, but present.

THE ARK: Peace didn't remove the pain, but it carried us through it.

CHAPTER 7

EVEN THOUGH, WE WILL

*Healing worship on ground
soaked by tears.*

This is an excerpt from a post I wrote on the day of Noah's memorial service.

Today was a day no parent plans for. Today was the day that we buried our son. Even though we had known this day was coming, nothing prepares you to step out of your car and walk toward a tiny casket. We chose today, March 13 (3/13), as an acknowledgment of Trisomy 13, the lethal genetic disorder that ended Noah's time here on earth. A disorder that we have learned far more about than we ever wanted to know. We have an intimacy with grief we never desired, yet we seek to honor it as an opportunity to serve others and deepen our healing. We have found that part of healing is helping.

Today, we wept deeply and worshiped intensely. We mourned his passing and celebrated his life. We acknowledged our pain and proclaimed victory over his story. We prayed over our family and friends, asking God to redeem Noah's life. We have prayed for so long that God would heal our son, and today we celebrated that answered prayer. We reminded ourselves that he won't return to us, but that one day we will go to him. Crushing sadness, yet indescribable peace. A truly bittersweet day. Hurting, but not hopeless. The more intense our grief, the more extravagant our worship. We declared over Noah's story a generational impact of rest found in salvation in Jesus Christ to reach far beyond what we could ever imagine. We continue to seek purpose for our pain. Even when it hurts, we boldly proclaim that God is still good. Even Though, We Will.

57.5 hours doesn't seem like much time, but today we celebrated every second, remembering the precious opportunity that we had to get to know our son and resting in his ultimate healing. We thanked God for the impact Noah is already having on our hearts and our community. We prayed with expectation for a greater impact yet to come. We are thankful that God is redeeming the story of our sweet son. In Jesus, nothing is without meaning, and nothing is beyond redemption.

We are thankful for the people God has put in our lives
to help prepare us for walking out this journey and to
carry us when we haven't had the strength to stand.
For the thousands of people praying for our young family,
we cannot express our gratitude enough. Please continue
as we strive to walk out this story. Many hard days are
ahead of us, but we take them one at a time. Join us in
praying for the redemption of Noah's story for God's glory.
May we rest in the arms of our Heavenly Father as
Noah rested in his earthly father's arms.

I will never forget that day. One of the harsh realities of Trisomy 13 is having to make arrangements for death while your child is still living in the womb. We found ourselves in a raw and confusing space: praying with confidence for healing while simultaneously being told we needed to make funeral arrangements for our son. Our doctor's office connected us with Athens Memory Garden, as they have an infant section on their grounds. I remember the cringe in my heart thinking of the other small tombstones that would surround my son. The devastation of sin in our world, that an entire section of a graveyard would be needed for infants. All of those families who had hurt so deeply. My hurting heart was going out to them. The staff was compassionate and helped us make arrangements remotely, as it was too hard for us to make ourselves go to sign the paperwork. Something about pulling onto the property where our son's earthly body would be laid to make final arrangements for his resting place was too high a hurdle for our young family at that time.

With that said, once the arrangements were made, I researched the flow of the property and the locations of the tiny headstones. I wanted to be prepared. My family needed me to lead in the midst of this battle, and I didn't feel like I could be effective without some kind of knowledge of where we were going. Learning this information on my terms felt comforting. Would we be on a hill? Would we be under tree cover or out in a field? Would it be a far walk from our car? What if Hannah has complications during the delivery, and I need to carry her? Will there be a place for her to sit? So much during this process was outside of my control, which flew in the face of my immature concept of leading my family.

Leading my family is not about control; it's about pointing them to the One who is in control, by humbly serving in every season. A couple of weeks before we would stand on the grounds and weep, I stood on the grounds and worshiped. We were in the area running some errands without Walker, and I told Hannah that I really needed to stop by as a step in preparing myself for what was to come. We drove around the area, and I stopped close to where we thought his body would lie. Hannah didn't want to get out of the car, so I kissed her head and stepped out. Little did we know that two weeks later, we would walk those exact same motions again.

On my solo journey gathering information, I walked the grounds and prayed. I saw the other tiny markers and prayed for their families. I looked at the open grassy space, and I cried. I listened to a song of worship and softly lifted my voice to Heaven. I was begging God to heal our son, and that one day I would get to bring him to this piece of land and talk about the miraculous work of our Savior. How we had purchased a spot to lay his earthly body, but God had another plan. I fiercely prayed with confident expectation that God had the means to write this part of the story. Before I left, I remembered Job and our mantra: Even Though, We Will. My faith is not built on this happening the way that I see fit. My faith is deeply rooted in my Salvation found in God through Jesus Christ. Before I left those grounds, I could feel my roots moving deeper. A peace came over me in the midst of my tears. God was going to heal my son on His terms, not mine. We prayed multiple times every day that God would heal our son and prepare our hearts for what was to come. While my hope was for the former in this moment, God's plan was for the latter. He had been preparing our hearts for more than 165 days, and on that ground on day 165, my roots went deeper, firming up my foundation.

The night before Noah's Memorial, Hannah had worked on making ribbons for everyone who was attending. In her normal fashion, she handled all of the details so effortlessly, making them so intentional. We bought yellow, green, and pink ribbons, the three colors of Trisomy 13 awareness. We had a small heart with Noah's name on the front and a pin to attach them to our clothes on the back. Our house had been quiet without our 18-month-old running around. We had been home alone for a few days, preparing ourselves for his service. We played music as we talked and cried. We wrote letters and shared stories of tender moments each of us got to spend with Noah. We were so thankful for the time we were able to spend with him. The night before his service carried an eerie stillness. A distinct closing of a chapter in Noah's life was taking place tomorrow morning. It was impossible to sleep knowing what lay in wait for us the next morning when we awoke.

The day of Noah's Memorial service was a blur. We had family and friends from out of town, sacrificially driving in. Everyone knew the address and the time we were supposed to arrive. Hannah and I got up after a restless night. It was quiet. We both showered and got dressed in nice spring clothes. Hannah had a thought prior to Noah's birth that I have since cherished. She wanted everyone to wear Spring clothes to Noah's Memorial. If we were to go to those grounds again, we would go with the focus that our son had been healed. In that spirit, we dressed and readied ourselves to leave the house. Each step seemed like an impossible undertaking as we drew nearer to the time we needed to leave.

Every mundane task of getting ready in the morning felt like a giant hurdle, inching us closer to those grounds. The time had finally come, so we got in the truck with our box full of ribbons. I prayed over our family before we pulled out of the driveway. We held hands, and through tears, we drove to his memorial service. I can still see the path we took that day when I close my eyes. I can see the turns, the stoplights, and even some of the cars that we passed. I often think of those people and pray for them. I don't know what kind of storm they were walking through, and I can't imagine trying to walk through it without my Savior and my community.

As we pulled onto the grounds, there was the dreaded green tent covering the hole the staff had dug in the ground. Hannah couldn't look, and I couldn't take my eyes off it. Slowly, we pulled the truck around and parked behind the other vehicles. Our friends and family were standing off to the side of the tent, quietly making conversation as some of them were meeting for the first time, while others were dear old friends. Everyone had respectfully followed our directions in wearing spring clothes. We both took a deep breath, and I turned the engine off.

Like last time, Hannah didn't want to get out of the car, so I kissed her head and stepped out. This time, I walked around to her door and opened it. She turned to me with tears in her eyes. I helped her out of the car and gave her a hug, whispering to her that I loved her and that she was my favorite. We walked hand in hand over to our friends and family, where many hugs and tears were shared by all. We handed out Noah's ribbons and prepared to sit underneath the tent. We learned something this day. In the midst of tragedy, the most meaningful thing you can offer is your presence. On this day, our friends and family understood there were no words to share to bring our son back. There were no words to share to make the pain in our hearts subside. Instead, there was the warmth of their embrace. A warmth that we so desperately needed. If you know someone in the midst of a tragedy, speak less and show up more. Your presence speaks louder and more clearly than words ever will.

For Noah's memorial service, we had asked our senior pastor to share some words of encouragement for the pain we were experiencing, and for two of our dear friends to sing. While I don't remember the words that were shared (sorry, Rob…), I will never forget the sounds of raw, raspy, snot-filled worship as we sang with friends and family. Music had been an anchor point for our souls during this season of grief and has continued to provide an avenue for healing. We sang two songs, *Another in the Fire* by Hillsong United and *Goodness of God* by Bethel Music. Songs that had been on repeat for months would take on a new meaning for our family in the next few moments of that dreadful day. The former speaks of several stories from the Bible where God showed up in the midst of a trial for His people. The story of Shadrach, Meshach, and Abednego being thrown into the fiery furnace, yet they were not alone, is the inspiration for the song title. We stood on ground soaked by tears, singing off-key, crying out to God, proclaiming that the grave is empty and we serve a Risen Savior who meets us in the midst of our mess. We were desperately seeking to find joy in the midst of our battle.

Our pastor shared, and I prayed over our young family. I prayed for many things, but one of them was that God would use our son's story for His glory. Little did we know the reach that Noah's story would have or how God would use our experience to help other hurting people. One day, I believe we will know more fully the reach in which God redeemed Noah's life and the hours that we were able to spend with him. On a relatively calm day, the wind began to blow, and the top of the tent opened up to allow the sun to shine through it. It was a gentle reminder of God's sovereign presence in the midst of every circumstance. The warmth on my tear-stained face seemed as if God was answering us with a "Just hold on for the ride."

The last song, Goodness of God, was another song that we had played on repeat for our family. I can remember singing out the first line, "*I love you, Lord, for your mercy never fails me,*" and not being able to speak another word. I cried. I prayed. I let our friends and family sing this over our wounded hearts. I said to myself multiple times, You are the same today as You were yesterday and as You will be tomorrow. Even Though, We Will. I believe in your unchanging character, even though I can't see it clearly right now. Then we got to the part of the song where they proclaim, "Your Goodness is running after me". I have never felt the presence of the Lord stronger than in this moment. I was encouraged, humbled, and awestruck at the tenderness of His embrace.

I helped Hannah back into the car and turned to walk back to the tent. As a dad, I desire to protect and lead my family by sacrificing myself. There was so little time to have done that for Noah. I wanted one last opportunity to fulfill my role as protector. While I knew that he wasn't still here in spirit, I honored his earthly body by helping them bury him. It was important to me that I see him through to his new resting place. The staff was very kind to let me be part of this intimate moment. They lifted his tiny casket off the cover and handed it to me to hold.

I sat with the casket in my lap as they prepared the grounds for it to rest.

I struggled to breathe.

I cried.

I prayed.

I was thankful that my sweet boy had been healed and that I would be able to see him again one day. My heart was aching, but it was rooted. My roots had already been prepared for this storm, and I was clinging tight to my Savior. No parent prepares to bury their child, but I was as prepared as I could be.

Standing at that graveside, I felt as though the world had stopped spinning. But over time, I began to see that while my world felt like it was falling apart, God had actually been holding the pieces of the calendar together in ways I couldn't have planned if I tried. Looking back, I can see a clear kindness in the timing of it all.

THE ARK: The more intense our grief, the more healing our worship.

CHAPTER 8

PERFECT TIMING

Seeing the kindness of God's plan in hindsight.

Looking back on Noah's birth and memorial service, we are reminded of God's timing. Noah was born at the start of the global COVID-19 pandemic that shut down our world in March of 2020. The day after we left the hospital, it issued a new COVID protocol that denied access to all visitors. He was born at a time that allowed our family and friends to be with our precious son and us. Likewise, our memorial service on March 13th was the last one that the funeral home held before shutting down for many months.

We know this was not everyone's experience, and we are forever grateful for the timing God allowed.

People say hindsight is always 20/20, but God's timing is not always clear. We trust that it is perfect, and sometimes that clarity comes quickly. Sometimes it's not as clear until months or years down the road. For Noah, we saw a clear kindness in the timing of his delivery. Noah was born the weekend before the hospital prevented any visitors. The memorial service was the last day they allowed services that spring.

All of the concerts and events we took Noah to in the womb that winter were cancelled through the spring and summer. Time with his grandparents would have been stripped away if he had been born later in March. All of the visitors who held and kissed him would have been turned away. The care and counsel we received from hospital staff and family would have been through a phone rather than face-to-face. The pandemic taught us many things, but one will always hold true: no matter how incredible the technology, you can never beat face-to-face. I cannot imagine walking through the journey without the people there to support us.

COVID brought its own struggles, but we were thankful for God's mercy in that wave not crashing over us before we went to the hospital.

THE ARK: Even when we can't see it,
God's timing is perfect.

CHAPTER 9

THE DASH

Measuring the weight of a life in the space between dates.

If timing is God's business, then the length of the 'dash' is His signature. We often focus on the dates that mark the beginning and the end, but God taught me to look at the space in between. It was a space I never imagined would be so short, yet so full.

Visiting Noah's Grave for the First Time

As a young father, I imagined seeing my children's names written in places like yearbooks, athletic programs, school play cast lists, and newspaper clippings. I am proud of the Efird name and prayed they would be too. I would beam with pride as I watched them grow and mature, discovering their individual gifting from the Lord. I would watch with love as Hannah taught them how to write their name and cherish the cards they made us, proudly signed in their own hand. I would laugh as I saw their name tagged on belongings they wanted to stake claim to from their siblings. Never, in all my daydreams of fatherhood, did I imagine seeing my son's name on a headstone.

At Noah's graveside, I was reminded of the weight carried by the dash of a life. His headstone marks the day he entered this world and the day he left it, but the dash holds something more. It holds the 57.5 hours we were given to hold him, sing to him, share him with friends and family, kiss him tenderly, and love him fiercely.

Our family continues to live within our dash: a life on mission, not yet fulfilling our role here. Our son Noah lived out his dash. His role here is complete, while ours carries on. Living within our dash, marked by the absence of one who no longer walks the journey with us, has been a delicate balancing act that we have struggled with since Noah went to be with Jesus. Now, we are living in the midst of adding additional dashes to our family story. All of our family's dashes will be unique, and I pray that they will be used for the glory of God. Even Though, We Will

I didn't know how I would react returning to his graveside for the first time since his memorial service. I've thought of this place often, yet have not had the strength to make the journey here. As I stood weeping over his grave, I was reminded that he's not in there. That small white casket that I helped lay into the cold, wet ground doesn't hold my son. I groaned aloud at the thought of my precious son being alone, cold, and abandoned, but his grave holds his earthly body; his Savior holds his eternal life. My prayers turned from sorrow to thanksgiving as I thanked my Heavenly Father for holding my sweet Noah tightly. When he passed from this side of eternity to the next, he went from his earthly father's arms into his Heavenly Father's arms, where he has been fully known and fully loved, completely cherished and whole.

The weight of loss and separation hung heavy on my shoulders, but I couldn't help but stand. I knelt to wipe off his headstone, but before I knew it, I found myself standing again. Warm, salty tears traced the well-worn paths of my face.

The dash holds the weight. The weight of a life is not measured by the dates on either end of the dash, but by what we do with the days held within it.

"Therefore take up the whole armor of God, that you may be able to withstand in the evil day, and having done all, to stand."

Ephesians 6:13 NKJV

In the presence of my son's grave, standing felt right. Not to look over him with disdain, but to stand in honor of his life.

To stand as a visual representation that our family is still standing.
To stand in silent applause for the time he fought to give his mother and me.
To stand as a reminder to myself that I am still called to lead and fight for my family, no matter the depth or breadth of our grief.

To stand with resolve.

We will stand.
Even Though, We Will.

"For we are His masterpiece, created in Christ Jesus for good works, which God prepared beforehand that we should walk in them."

Ephesians 2:10 NKJV

The verse on Noah's headstone was imprinted into my heart during college, unaware of what stood in the path of my life. I was enthralled with God's ability to redeem our story for His glory. Little did I know the depth of His redemption nor the weight of His sovereign plan. I am regularly amazed at how God gives us people, verses, songs, and stories not for the moment but in preparation for what the future holds.

Today, I am hurting, but hopeful. Hurting for the scarce number of memories we will have to cherish of our son, Noah. Hopeful that I will one day soon see him again, made whole in the presence of our Savior. It is to this hope that we cling. We will cherish his life, his name, and his dash. Oh my sweet boy, I long to see you again one day. I pray that we honor your dash. Your mother and I are seeking to invest the days in our dash well, but it too will end. May we be good stewards of our time here. Until then, we will stand.

Even Though, We Will

THE ARK: We don't solve grief, we learn to carry it by living inside the dash.

CHAPTER 10

LIVING WITH GRIEF

Learning to walk in the presence of remembered pain.

A dash: the sum of our life displayed in stone for all to see. What will we do with that dash?

Noah's dash consisted of 57.5 hours. A brief span by earthly measure, yet immeasurable in weight. When redeemed by God, that dash is no longer confined to breath and time; it opens into eternity.

Below is a raw journal entry as our hearts ached. The weighted bear that meant so much to our family.

One Month.

That's how old Noah would have been today. Grief alters the reality of time. Some days inch by painfully slow, like a child waiting for Christmas. Other days race by like a movie on fast forward, appearing as blurred scenes of faces and emotions that never fully settle. It took me until almost dinner time to realize the significance of this day. My sweet bride had to gently remind me. We were given a bear embroidered with Noah's name, weighted to match his birth weight. It sat at the foot of our bed for days, untouched. Neither of us had the mental capacity or emotional endurance to open it. Tonight, we hesitatingly opened that package. The feeling of the soft hair and the weight was a bittersweet moment. There is a specific, hollow ache in a parent's arms when they go from holding a child every second to holding nothing at all. That 5lb 5oz weight was a physical anchor for my soul. It didn't replace Noah, but it gave my body a way to process the gravity of his absence when my mind was too tired to find the words.

We let Walker hold Noah's bear, and his tender embrace was like that at the hospital. Such a good big brother he was and would have continued to be. It will be something that we use to help him process the passing of his younger brother, but for now, it's Noah's bear that he gets to hug and sleep with.

We live in the presence of remembered pain. Remembering memories that already seem to be fading in clarity, of holding, kissing, singing, snuggling, loving. A pain that forces us to acknowledge the absence of our son. A pain that confronts our sadness of missing our sweet boy. An intense pain unlike anything we have ever experienced. A pain that seems as if it's every bit a member of our family as Noah. The intensity of our pain is matched by the depth of our love. Early on, a new and cherished friend told me, "Every lament is a love story". We don't fear emotions. Emotions, in themselves, are healthy. We fear that we won't process them in a healthy way. We fear that we won't allow ourselves to go into the pit of our pain to find its depth, because at that depth, we can find a starting point for our healing. We have stopped telling people that we are okay, because truly, we aren't. We are hurting, deeply wounded by the reality that today would have been a day of celebration with pictures of Noah in a cute outfit, with a #1 beside him, and some catchy saying like "Praise the Lord for coffee."

Somehow, we subconsciously thought that time would stand still in the presence of our reality, yet the world moves on, as it has each day until now and will until Jesus returns. A stopping of time would allow us to relish in the nearness of our son, because the more time that passes, the further we get from having held him. If we allow ourselves, this separation can be all-consuming. Yet, it means that each day we get further from holding him here means we get one day closer to holding him in eternity. Perspective matters in grief. Our minds default to the path of least resistance, the one well trodden with anxiety, depression, loneliness, abandonment, and hopelessness. Self-loathing and self-pity are still rooted in the self. While we hurt, while we struggle, while we miss, we can't overlook the emotions of ourselves, but we must turn our gaze to Jesus, the author and perfecter of our faith.

We are learning to welcome our emotions, feebly attempting to process them in the presence of God's grace and mercy, and seeking to navigate through them as we desperately miss our son and desire to honor his life. We find ourselves regularly praying and worshiping, not because we are super Christians, but rather because we intimately know the weight of our suffering. A suffocating weight mentally, physically, and emotionally. Prayer and worship provide a reprieve, not to be normal, but to stand and breathe. Normal has lost its meaning for our family. Yet even now, Even Though, We Will.

We will leverage the tender presence of God in our lives to take one step at a time. A necessity that we won't always hold, but that we will look back on these days, thanking God for His faithfulness to not leave us nor to be afraid of the depth of our pain. A depth that our Heavenly Father intimately knows. Being Easter week, we are thankful for Jesus' sacrifice on the cross for our sins, providing a way for us to be reunited with our son one day. Until that day, we will strive to glorify God our Father and honor the life of our second son, Noah.

Everyone loves the story of a hero, using their abilities to fight for those without them. We seek to fight for the honor of our son, who can no longer fight for himself, but not under our own frail strength. We fight surrounded by a great cloud of witnesses, of family, friends, colleagues, and total strangers, lifting our mourning family up with thoughts and prayers. We know that God's goodness and mercy are pursuing us, even in the midst of our suffering. Every wound heals with proper attention and time, leaving a scar that tells the story of pain and redemption. That scar will be evident in our young family. We love our sweet boy. We miss him deeply. We are hurting, but healing, one day at a time. We covet your thoughts and prayers; they carry us each step of our day. May we all find rest in the presence of our Savior, Jesus Christ.

We were learning to live in the dash, not trying to solve it.

THE ARK: The weight of our pain is matched by the depth of our love, and God meets us in the dash between them.

CHAPTER 11

WHEN GRIEF HAS NO ENERGY

Why God does not confuse exhaustion with disobedience.

Grief doesn't always cry. Sometimes it goes quiet.

In our story, we found that mental fog affected every aspect of our lives. We would forget important dates and leave text messages unread. Every day, household items were regularly misplaced. Packages sat unopened on the table for days. Naps were not a luxury but a requirement.

Our brains felt like an old computer with too many tabs open. It was very frustrating. Simple tasks felt overwhelming. Future plans were impossible to wrap our heads around. Easy choices took very intentional focus.

Normal had lost its meaning for our family. I remember asking myself, "Am I letting God down because I can't seem to function?" Here is a truth I had to digest. God is not disappointed by your limits; He designed you with them. When we rest, we are living out a foundational truth that He is in control. We know He is still running the universe even when we aren't awake to "help". Rest is not surrendering to grief; it is a proclamation of trust in the One who never slumbers. He does not confuse exhaustion with disobedience. The body was not designed to carry this much loss without rest.

If you find yourself in this season, please know that rest does not equal unfaithfulness. Survival is not apathy. During this season, routines will change. Responsibilities need to be minimized. There is no schedule for grief, and your energy will return at uneven intervals.

THE ARK: Take a nap and learn to say No, both will be vital in this season.

If you love someone in this season, you will need to know that a person in the waves of grief doesn't have the energy to respond to every text or call. It isn't personal. They are in extreme triage, and they are choosing to get out of bed today. That choice takes energy, mental capacity, and willpower. That effort will take precedence over responding to you. They still love you and appreciate the thoughts and prayers. Give them grace when it seems as though they are ignoring you.

We don't solve grief; we learn to carry it by living inside the dash.

THE ARK: God is not disappointed by your limits; He designed you with them.

CHAPTER 12

BIRTHDAYS WITHOUT YOU

Cupcakes and Missing Memories.

On Noah's second birthday, I wrote:

Happy 2nd birthday to our precious son, Noah. Today is a day full of competing emotions. Today is a day that we cherish and mourn.

We cherish the life of our sweet Noah. We cherish the miraculous 57.5 hours that we got to spend with him. We cherish his strength and the fierceness in his eyes. We cherish the pictures. We cherish the friends and family who got to hold him. We cherish the memories, even as they seem to slowly fade. We cherish the ability to share his story and our family's journey. We cherish the empathy we have for others, especially those hurting in the midst of the passing of a loved one.

We mourn his absence. The absence of more memories. The absence of hugs, kisses, and laughter. The absence of first steps and snotty noses. The absence of cuddles and wrestling. The absence of family pictures. The absence of the routine of having three young boys at home. The absence of teeth to brush and boo-boos to kiss. The absence of matching jammies and family movie nights. The absence of favorite foods and ticklish spots. The absence of an extra car seat and an extra pair of shoes by the door. The physical absence of his sweet, strong presence in our daily life.

Today is bittersweet. Bitter in that the absence reminds us of the hole in our hearts. Sweet in that we cherish knowing our precious son is fully healed in the presence of our Savior, awaiting our arrival. Bitter in that the warm salty tears still stain our faces like they did the day we first found out about his diagnosis. Sweet in that we were able to cherish so much more time with him than we had anticipated. Bitter in that today is not filled with cake, friends, and laughter. Sweet in that we value our time together as a family more deeply. Bitter in that our son has a grave and a headstone. Sweet in that his final resting place isn't in the ground in that tiny casket. Bitter in that our family intimately knows the depth of despair in death. Sweet in that death is not the final chapter. Bitter in that our family will forever be scarred by his absence. Sweet in that our family will forever be sealed by the promise that we will be able to cherish time together again one day soon.

Thank you to all of you who have prayed for our family, sent letters, texts, emails, food, or served as a listening ear. We are better today because of your love in action towards our family. We are prayerful about how God will continue to use our family's story and Noah's life to help others, more of which we will share in the coming months. But for today, we cherish and mourn.

Even Though, We Will

On Noah's third birthday, I wrote the following:

The weight of death is carried by those left behind to live on the other side of loss, and today my shoulders are trembling. Noah, my sweet son, I miss you. My grieving, aching heart longs to be with you. I know that you are not lost, but in the arms of our Savior, even though the void left in your absence is the most tragic loss. I know I will see you again, but the waiting seems like an insurmountable obstacle this year, as you would have been three today. I know that as my tears fall down the well-worn paths on my face, one day my mourning will turn to dancing.

Today is a day that I'm reminded of all the things we will miss with you. No terrible twos tantrums. Oh, how I wish I could hear you scream. No trying threes awaiting you, on this, your third birthday. No snuggles with younger brothers. No wrestling with daddo and older brother. No first fishing trips or favorite candy. What would your voice sound like? What would your hugs feel like? What would be your favorite book to have me read? What would have been your first words? Would you be a momma's boy or a dad-o's warrior? What would your cry sound like? Would your laugh fill a room, or would you try to hide it in clenched teeth? Would you be very outgoing like dad, or prefer smaller groups like mom?

In the quietness of the early morning, with closed eyes and a prayerfully focused mind, I can smell your sweet smell as if I were still holding you. I can hold my arms in such a way to remember lovingly embracing your tiny body. I can strain to see the depth in your eyes as if my gaze were still transfixed on them. A grieving dad, navigating life without all of his warriors in tow. A life lived without a multitude of experiences. Oh my sweet boy, I grieve the missing memories.

My precious son, I try to take comfort in the pains you will never see. You never experienced heartbreak. You will never have to know the sting of death or the pain from this broken world. You will never have a broken bone or a skinned knee. You will never have a cavity or a stomach bug. While you have so many nevers, we hold the most damaging: we will never again have you to hold and grow with on this side of eternity. Only our memories that we fight to hold onto.

Nothing prepares a parent to bury their child. Even more unprepared is life after the funeral. There is a crushing, numbing vastness to the void felt in our hearts. Time heals a multitude of wounds, but not this one. There is no complete healing this side of eternity. Tears still flow, and our hearts still ache. How do we talk about you? How do we kindly correct random people on how many kids we have? We try to bring you up in conversation to celebrate your life without offloading the weight of your absence on unsuspecting bystanders. We have found ways to share your story and God's faithfulness through it all. We are reminded of His Poema (masterpiece). You were fearfully and wonderfully made. You were created in Christ Jesus for Good works. You were knit together in mommy's womb. You were not a mistake. You are still a wonderful, cherished member of our family.

Today, we started a new tradition of making cupcakes to celebrate Noah's birthday. A cupcake is small and sweet, like Noah. We will try to find new flavors each year, intentionally marking a new experience for our family in celebrating his life. Today's cupcake was funfetti, being that each one is fully unique, like our sweet Noah.

On days like today, especially like today, I mourn the vast sea of experiences we never had. I will long to find comfort in our reunion one day. Today, I fight to celebrate your precious life, full of the 57.5 hours that we were blessed to spend with you, such a tender gift. While my shoulders tremble, they will not falter. Today, I fight to honor your life. Today, I choose to continue to fight for your mom and your brothers. Today, we honor you. Happy 3rd birthday, precious boy.

We miss you dearly. We love you completely. We thank God for your life. We long to see you again.

Until then, Even Though, We Will

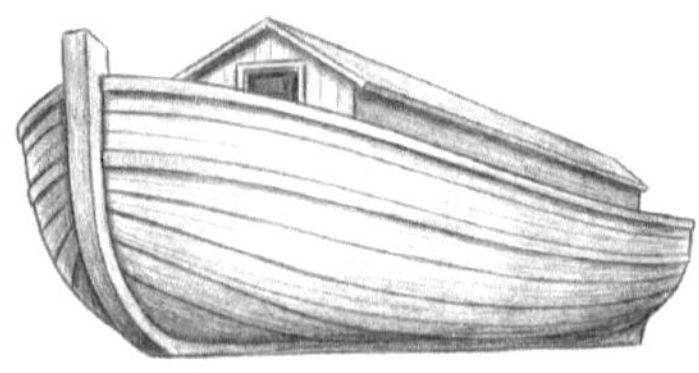

THE ARK: Grief holds both love and
absence at the same time.

CHAPTER 13

A DELICATE DANCE

Finding the rhythm of worshiping and weeping.

We sought not to move past our grief too quickly, afraid to dishonor the value of the life of our son. Yet, we desired not to sit in our grief in self-pity and self-deprecation, not rising to see the sun. Our mourning would be turned to dancing, but this dance was a delicate one. One with tender memories and intense pain. It's easy to be in the presence of one, while also feeling guilty that it's not the other.

Sad but peaceful described many days after that. Grief hits in waves, some that would sweep you off your feet and hold you under. I can remember playing in the ocean as a young boy, and a big wave would crest on top of us, knocking us down to the sand below. Our dad, much taller and stronger than we, would tenderly wrap his arms around us, picking us up. We would hold our breath, longing for the embrace of our dad. When grief hit, it was our Heavenly Father that we ran to. We longed for His embrace and for His presence.

Confidence is built, and rest is found in the presence of loving strength. We found that music spoke deeply to our souls, so we played music regularly. We declared promises over our family in word, in music, in writing, and in quiet prayer. There is a rhythm found throughout the Psalms of intense worship and intense lament; I call them worshiping and weeping. Entire Psalms are dedicated to worship and to weeping, while others oscillate between both, like Psalm 13. This truth gave us comfort and hope for the emotions we were experiencing. David was a man after God's own heart (Acts 13:22), so we felt as if we were in good company.

THE ARK: Healing is not abrupt or triumphant; it is careful and costly.

CHAPTER 14

EMBRACING THE HARD

Moving forward one step at a time.

Hard.

Sometimes that was the only word I could bring myself to type.

I think it defines what we are trying to do, something hard.

We have been stumbling up the hill of grief, one day at a time. Grief gives us the greatest excuse to take the easy way out. In our lives, marriage, parenting, health, relationships, and work.

I haven't always gotten this right since Noah died, and I've found myself playing the victim card far too often by choosing the easy way out. Today, I'm determined to honor the strength of our precious Noah by pursuing what is Hard.

We had a good friend help us create a workout to honor and remember Noah's strength while also committing to building our own. A workout designed with the fingerprint of Noah.

> *"Noah Clifton"*
>
> *13 rounds*
>
> *3 deadlifts 255/175*
>
> *5 strict pull-ups*
>
> *7 push-ups*
>
> *20 sit-ups*
>
> *57.5 FT walking lunge*

13 rounds of hard work to draw our focus on the extra 13th chromosome that he fought hard against his entire life.

57.5 feet to honor each hour his earthly body held breath.

5 pull-ups and 5 body-weight movements, remembering the strength of his 5 lb 5 oz body.

3, 7, and 20, representing his birthday, the day we were privileged to hold a strong, brave, fighting, beautiful member of our family.

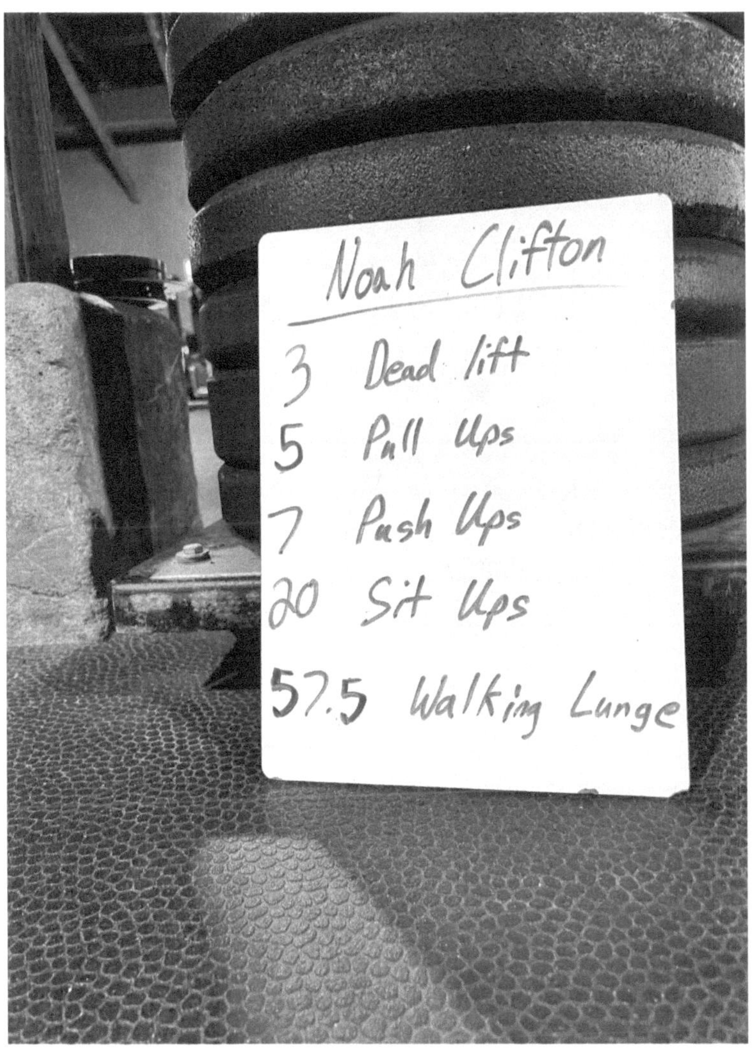

We quickly learned during our first time through the workout that hard won't be perfect. In CrossFit, doing a workout as written is called Rx'd, meaning no changes and no shortcuts. If you are like me, most days, just getting through the round is the victory. Whether you're in a gym or just trying to get through a Tuesday without breaking down, doing the 'hard' thing doesn't always look like the original plan; it looks like refusing to quit.

Hannah and I both wanted to Rx our first workout, but were unable to. Instead of taking the easy route, we chose modifications that pushed us to our limits. And then we put our heads down and started moving until the hard work was completed.

THE ARK: Don't allow your grief to confuse you into thinking the easy way is the best way. Choose to do the right thing, especially when it's hard.

My prayer is that this will be a defining example for our family; no matter how hard or how slow progress may be, it's worth moving forward one step at a time, with our eyes fixed on Jesus. This resolve reminds me of something we say at church:

> *In the midst of the storm, look over at the sleeping Jesus. He knows the storm is coming. He is confident in His power. Keep your eyes on Jesus. He's in the midst of the storm with you.*

My precious son, I choose once again to step into the Hard today with my eyes on Jesus. I am a better man because of you. I love you, Noah. Another year closer to seeing you again. Until then, may I follow your example and step into the Hard while there is still breath in my lungs.

THE ARK: Grief gives excuses to quit, but love
calls us forward.

CHAPTER 15

THE MERCY I DIDN'T EXPECT

The gift of being fully present for a life.

Today would have been Noah's 5th birthday, a whole hand. What I would give for just a few moments more. If only I could be planning a surprise birthday party for him this morning, waiting to hear his hearty laugh as he runs down the stairs, and feel the warmth of his small yet strong embrace. Today, where there should be high fives, too much sugar, and lots of presents, there will be gentle embraces, countless tears, and a few cupcakes shared by those left in the waiting.

I long for the time when there will be no more separation and time will not be a factor, but in the lingering, my soul aches. Each day, I wrestle with moving farther away from his earthly memory and closer to his heavenly reunion. Some days, my focus is drawn back to the hospital room, fighting to replay every moment from every hour we spent with him. Then, other days, my focus is drawn up to the eventual embrace when we are reunited in eternity.

We long to see him. We fight to remember the softness of his skin, the depth of color in his eyes, and the sweet smell of his thick hair. I dream of what his voice will sound like and which of his brothers he would be most like. Would he be as thought-provoking as Walker, as tender-hearted as Abel, or a joy tornado like Warren? Would red or green be his favorite color? Would he cheer for UGA? Would he be one to instigate or mediate fights with his brothers?

A dear friend once told me, "Grief keeps you at the grave. Mourning moves you forward." Today, I mourn all the things Noah and I missed out on. The high school prom awkwardness. Who would he have taken? The first time driving away from the house as a 16-year-old. Would he be a car or a truck guy? The cracking of his voice as he moved through puberty. Would he be embarrassed or embrace it? The father-son trip when he turned 10. What would he be so enamored with that it's obvious where we would go? The look on his face when he begins to read. Which story would be the one that we can quote to him because we read it so many times? The relief on Hannah's and my faces when he finally mastered potty training. How many times would we be needed to clean up accidents? But it's mainly the joy he would have brought into our family's life. There's so much we've learned from Noah's life, but there's so much that we miss. The mark he left on our family could have been so much different.

In moments of clarity, I am also reminded of all the things he didn't have to experience. The feeling of burning your hand on a hot stove. The sharp pain of breaking a bone. The overwhelming heartache when your heart gets broken for the first time. The way poison ivy itches. The way a close friend lets you down. The pain of rejection. The fear of not being enough. The scars that words can cause. The disappointment of his sinful dad not getting it all right.

As a husband, dad, and leader, my default setting is problem solver. If Hannah or the boys are hurting, I want to stand between them and the pain. But you can't tackle a chromosome. You can't outwork a terminal diagnosis. For months, I felt like a failure because I couldn't protect Noah. But in those 57.5 hours, God changed my view of protection.

I have been blessed with four amazing sons, but Noah is the only one that I didn't let down. He never heard me raise my voice or lose my temper. I never had to discipline him. I didn't miss a moment of his life. All 57.5 hours of his dash, between March 7, 2020, and March 9,

2020, I was fully present. As he took his final breath on this side of eternity, the final words he heard were me saying, "I love you." He went to sleep in the arms of his earthly father and woke up in the arms of his Heavenly Father. I can't say that for anyone else in my life, but I can say it of Noah. What a gift in the midst of such a tragedy. What a merciful God we serve.

This March 2020 journal entry describes a perspective shift that has been powerful for me. In this life, each of us is promised trials and suffering. As parents, we would gladly take this suffering from any of our children. For Noah, we were allowed to do that. We were allowed to experience all of his suffering. Even as a flawed Dad, I would carry this burden for any of my children.

THE ARK: Carry the weight of suffering
for your loved ones.

I know that this isn't everyone's story. We watch as our children suffer, and we beg God to allow us to carry that weight for them. But in Noah's story, we were uniquely gifted with this ability. The weight was crushing, but I would carry it without question for any of my family. It makes me think of our Savior, Jesus Christ. He chose to carry our burden. The burden of sin should have nailed you and me to the cross. But God, who is RICH in Mercy, took our place. It was my sin that held Him there. And He would do it again, because of His love for you and me.

I will continue to fight the battle of choosing to celebrate Noah's life and the impact it has made, and is yet to make, in so many lives. I don't always understand the ways of the Lord, but in Him, I trust. I find peace even in the presence of such pain. My precious son, Happy Birthday. I am a better man, husband, father, and leader because of you. Here's to honoring your life, one day at a time. Your mom and I love you. We will see you soon.

THE ARK: Both sorrow and thankfulness can be true at the same time.

CHAPTER 16

LITTLE REDEEMING MOMENTS

Precious conversations with big brothers.

We continue to find redeeming moments with our family. The following is a journal entry from the first time Walker visited Noah's graveside with me. It was a lesson in broken blueprints.

Over six and a half years ago, when I learned I was going to be a dad, I never dreamed of a scenario like today. Bittersweet. A piercing, soul-aching bitterness accompanied by an unexplainable, gentle, tender, awe-inspiring sweetness. I took my oldest son to visit the grave of his younger brother...

Today, while running an errand with Walker, we passed by Noah's grave. I mentioned to him that his brother Noah's body was buried there. He asked if we could stop by on our way home. As I said yes, tears welled in my eyes, and that old familiar knot returned to my throat. Was I a bad dad that I hadn't brought Walker here almost three and a half years later? Would I be able to get out of the vehicle? Would it be too emotional for Walker? What if it were a moment God was planning to redeem, would I trust Him to step into it?

The next thirty minutes produced the most precious and painful conversation with our bright young son. Only God can redeem our darkest moments. Mercy is present in the midst of tragedy. The value of time and space to grieve. The healing powers of tears, friends, and laughter. Sadness, tears, and emotions don't make you less than; they make you more fully human, as God designed. The reason why our souls long for worship music and how it combats the crushing weight of death. All in, our need for a Savior.

I shared our assurance that Noah is with Jesus, an answer to so many prayers for healing. And a short yet detailed biology lesson on trisomy 13, because Walker is an ever-curious child with an ironclad memory who doesn't take "because I said so" as an answer. Explaining a "broken blueprint" to a young son is a delicate balance, but I tried to choose words that would honor both the reality of his diagnosis and the sanctity of his life. I wanted Walker to understand that while Noah's body didn't work the way ours did, he was still fearfully and wonderfully made.

It was hard to describe to him the intensity with which his mother and I prayed for Noah's healing. While sharing with my oldest son, the one who made me a dad, that my faith is what gives me hope for the future, even when it doesn't make sense, he asked several heartfelt questions. I shared that I don't always get it right and I don't always know the answers, but here's what I know for sure: Jesus is the same today as He was yesterday and as He will be tomorrow, and He is my Savior, and His Saving Grace is available to all of us. Then we arrived at our errand's destination, and our conversation turned to the task at hand. I didn't know if he would remember his desire to stop or not, so I didn't bring it up again.

As soon as we got back in the truck, he asked if I was going to take him to Noah's grave. Maybe it was the hope that he would get to see him. Or maybe it was the fact that we had spent a great extended weekend with dear friends who have a son the age that Noah would be, but Walker was determined to stop by. The absence of Noah's presence in the truck felt more tangibly real as we drove ever closer to his body's resting place.

As we pulled into a place that holds such intense emotions for our family, Walker asked how I remembered where I was going. Choked up, I struggled to get out the words that I will never forget this place. As a father, my desire and calling is to serve and protect my family. This place saw the end of that watch for sweet Noah. I fought to tell him about the day of his memorial service and the friends and family that stood alongside us that day and cried, sang, and embraced.

We got out and walked over to a small area within the memorial grounds. An area full of more little gravestones than when I last visited. An area representing many crushed families struggling to hold onto the memories of their tiny loved ones. Tiny in size, but massive in impact.

Then we came to Noah's. We stood quietly and looked, then I read Walker the wording. We both shared how much we missed Noah. I tried to describe the things I remember about him and to reassure Walker that he isn't in that ground. By bringing Walker here, I wasn't keeping him stuck in the past; I was inviting him into our family's full story. We've learned that redemption doesn't mean we stop talking about the one who is gone.

We hugged and snapped a picture. Then we were off to look around and read the other headstones. In between, Walker would ask questions.

I don't know why God chose to heal our sweet Noah on the other side of eternity, but today I'm thankful for how

He is redeeming Noah's story in the life of his brother and his dad. Until we meet again, my heart aches for your embrace. May we continue to honor your precious life as we live out ours.

THE ARK: Redemption does not erase the darkness; it enters it.

A TESTIMONY OF TRUST

Why continuing to live is not a betrayal of the one who is gone.

We never felt that our family was complete when we had Walker or when we became pregnant with Noah. Then we received Noah's diagnosis, and we both felt unwilling to speak of the future. We wanted to be fully present for the time we would have with Noah and circle back to the future later. We were navigating the grief of one son being in heaven and the uncertainty of a pandemic alongside a rambunctious two-year-old toddler. Neither of us wanted to approach the topic of getting pregnant again, but something that we had learned through our grief is that continuing to take steps together as a family is not disrespectful to our sweet Noah. Rather, we are honoring his life by continuing to pursue God with ours.

Along the way, we had many conversations about how we would honor Noah. Part of honoring him meant learning how to keep living without pretending we weren't grieving.

We would get asked at the grocery store, when someone saw Walker, "Oh, when are you going to have another?" Or "He sure could use a baby brother or sister to play with, why don't y'all get on that?" In this moment, do I unload the depth of our grief on this well-meaning elderly lady who simply loves seeing the joys of children in the midst of a loving family? Or do I smile and say, "Thanks"?

Some days, we would get asked while together, and we would just look at each other, almost as if to say, "you're up." One of us would take over the conversation, either detailing the recent events of our family and Noah's residence in heaven, or by saying that we were continuing to pray about it. We quickly found that the former could be used like a club, beating people over the head. We had a deep desire not to make our grief about ourselves.

I have found that telling people we have four children, three here with us, is an easy way to bridge this gap. Likewise, when I share the ages of our sons, I always try to include how old Noah would have been. I say something like, "Walker is eight, Noah would have been six, Abel is five, and Warren is three."

By doing these two things, I am able to acknowledge him as a member of our family and leave the door open should the individual want to ask further questions. Not everyone wants to talk about your grief and that's okay. By using this approach, you leave the door open should they want to step into that conversation.

THE ARK: Acknowledge every member of your family, including those in Heaven, when sharing your story with others.

In our pursuit of God, we felt called to continue growing our family. We prayed individually as well as together for His will to be made clear in our lives. We had to be honest with each other: another child wouldn't be a 'replacement' for Noah. This fear is so valid for anyone who has experienced child loss. We found speaking it out loud and praying against it helped us fight this temptation. This replacement temptation causes a couple of serious issues. First, we don't ever fully process the grief from the passing of a child. Second, we immediately set the next child up for failure, holding them to an expectation to heal our hurting hearts. No one outside of the person of Jesus Christ can fill this void! We realized that our love for Noah didn't have a limit that would be reached if we had more children. Instead, his life had increased our capacity to love the kids God would eventually bring into our home.

We were united in trusting His plans for our lives, even though we were nervous about growing our family biologically again. Although a small increase, we were at a greater risk of having another Trisomy 13 child after having Noah. Likewise, so many other complications can come up, some of which you may have personally experienced. God was merciful in giving us unity in a desire to continue to grow our family biologically.

This took time and intentionality from each of us. Ultimately, it took trusting in our Heavenly Father. Because we trusted His plans, we now have four amazing boys! While Walker was our firstborn and Noah our second, God in His mercy eventually brought Abel and Warren into our family. They are not 're-placements' for the brother who is waiting for them in Heaven. They are new, beautiful dashes in our family story. Their infectious laughter and captivating smiles are a testimony that even though the storm was real, life, abundant life, continues to grow on this side of the waves.

Within grief, it's easy to get stuck in the rut of self-pity and even self-loathing. We didn't want to hide our grief or be scared of it, but we also didn't want to make others around us feel that they had to be joyless around us. My grief shouldn't prevent your joy. Sadly, we've all been around people like this. They are so miserable in their individual life that being around them is like being around a vacuum that is sucking the very energy out of you. Was our grief easy to walk through? Of course not! But we also constantly sought to engage with the good around us through our friends and family. This engagement with good helped us fight off deep anxiety and depression. Grief is a dense fog that shades every area of your life. If you allow it, grief can give you the false sense that everything in life is the same stale gray.

We felt such guilt when we were frustrated with our oldest son, Walker, who was healthy and navigating the emotions of the Trying Twos. How could we ever get upset with him? He was healthy and still breathing. The miracle of life, yet we often found ourselves on the verge of losing our emotional cool. Satan really attacked us as a couple in this arena, a battlefront we hadn't originally planned to fight on. And yet, we chose to fight. We prayed over Walker more fervently and recruited many dear friends to do the same. Loss is difficult for everyone in the family. We wanted to honor Noah's life while still cherishing Walker's. Only a parent who has lost a child will understand the struggle, yet it is a key area for anyone you know who is navigating these treacherous waters will need continuous prayer.

If you find yourself trying to love someone through their grief, focus on two things: 1) show up and 2) ask questions. We found that people who were willing to sit with us in our sadness were vital to our survival. They would ask questions about Noah and our family. Then, they would listen, giving us the freedom to share or to be silent. That's it. It doesn't take a perfectly crafted statement, but it does take you out of your comfort zone. Allow them to ask questions without feeling the need to answer them. Presence is greater than words here.

THE ARK: Continuing to live is not a betrayal; it is a testimony.

CHAPTER 18

A T-SHIRT IS WORTH A THOUSAND WORDS

Wearing the battle cry of our family.

The shirt we shared with those who stood beside us at Noah's memorial service.

We included this letter with Noah's shirt for those who stood beside us in our earliest days of grief.

A heartfelt thank you seems to fall short of the depth of our gratitude for you and the way you have loved our family, but we wanted to take the opportunity to express how thankful we are. Thank you for being with us in our most difficult days. Thank you for your prayers both then and now. Thank you for your hugs and tears. Thank you for the thoughtful cards and delicious meals. Thank you for being a listening ear. Thank you for standing with us as we honored our sweet Noah's life. Thank you for fighting alongside us to honor and remember Noah's life.

We had this design made to help tell the story of our journey. His name is centered at the top, accompanied by two dates. The date on the left is his birthday. The date on the right is the date that he went to be with Jesus. The phrase at the bottom, "Even Though, We Will," became the battle cry of our family. We chose, and still choose, to believe that God is in control, that His perfect plans don't always make sense to us, and that we will trust His unchanging character.

The road leading between the dark mountains down into the valley notes our walk into the depths of mourning and loss.

Psalm 23:4 says, "Though I walk through the valley of the shadow of death, I will fear no evil, for You are with me." As the backdrop of the design, we want to be reminded that even in the darkest nights, we are never alone.

The path itself has the word Poema engraved on it. Poema is the Greek word for masterpiece, found in Ephesians 2:10 (which we had engraved on Noah's headstone). We want to be reminded that the road that we walked with Noah's life was not by mistake. Jesus is creating something in us for our good and for His Glory. Furthermore, Noah's life was not a mistake but a masterpiece created in Christ Jesus. One day, we will get to celebrate face-to-face with him again.

Finally, the ark. Noah's ark serves as a reminder of how, in Genesis, God made a way to carry Noah and his family through the flood. He didn't remove them from the storm, but He carried them through it. We want to be reminded that being in a storm doesn't mean that we have been abandoned by God. Throughout our entire journey with our sweet Noah, God was and has been with us, holding the doors shut to keep out the raging seas.

We will be using this design and shirts like this as an opportunity to raise money for a foundation we are creating in Noah's honor. We have found that a large part of our healing process is sharing our story with others who are hurting. There was so little we could do in Noah's journey, but his foundation helps to give our family a path to work out our healing. A way to find purpose in our pain in helping others.

The foundation's first focus will be sending care packages to families that have received a diagnosis of Trisomy 13. The care packages will be called Noah's Arks. They will include things we found to be helpful in the lead-up to and post-hospital trip, as well as prayers from our family. These Arks include the same anchors that held us: a candle for a comforting smell; high-quality journals for the mental fog; games for the family to enjoy together; and gift cards to local restaurant chains for when making dinner is too great a task. We want these families to have something they can touch and feel while they navigate the unseen.

We had these specific shirts made for those who stood beside us at Noah's memorial service. Thank you for making your love tangible for our family. We hope that this shirt will encourage you in your walk with the Lord and remind you of our sweet Noah.

THE ARK: God may not remove the flood,
but He never leaves the boat.

PART TWO

THE FOUNDATIONAL GROUND

The Theology We Had to Fight For

At some point, the question shifts from "How do I survive today?" to "Is there anything solid left to stand on?"

These chapters are our honest attempt to find out. We did not arrive at neat answers. We arrived at bedrock: something firm enough to hold the full weight of our grief.

If you are still underwater, come back to this section later. It will be here.

CHAPTER 19

WHEN GOD DOESN'T EXPLAIN HIMSELF

Trusting the character of the Maker.

I used to think I had an answer for most everything. As a leader and a business owner, I was regularly in positions to solve problems and provide clarity. But on September 17th, when our doctor uttered 'abnormalities,' my library of answers vanished in an instant. I didn't need a lecture on theology; I needed to know why my son's heart had holes in it. Before we look at the 'why' of suffering, I have to be honest: this wasn't a theological exercise for me. It was a cry from my heart in the driver's seat of my truck with my head against the steering wheel.

We've been asked so many times why God allows bad things to happen. Below is my attempt at answering this for our family.

This question wasn't a theological exercise; it was a deeply personal one, asked from the middle of the waves of our storm rather than from the safety of the shore.

As a parent, you eventually get to a place where you just want your child to trust you and act on your request. I want you to trust that my past faithfulness aligns with my current request. My love for you undergirds the request I am making.

Say Walker is running around the house in his favorite socks, but they're slick on the bottom. If he keeps running around the table, he's going to fall, just like he has many times in the last few weeks. So what does a loving father do? I remove the socks from his feet so he can run with more traction. He cries, only seeing the thing he wants, his socks, and not the whole picture. From an early age, we struggle with trusting others. We put confidence in our ability to reason and understand what is happening. Our ability to create and conquer. And when those abilities fail us, frustration often turns into distrust.

We all need to pause as we continue on our grief journey. Scripture doesn't dismiss our questions, but it does reorient them.

> *"For My thoughts are not your thoughts, Nor are your ways My ways," says the Lord. "For as the heavens are higher than the earth, so are My ways higher than your ways, And My thoughts than your thoughts."*
>
> *Isaiah 55:8-9 NKJV*

If we allow ourselves to admit that we don't have everything figured out, we can engage this question both theologically and with an honest, aching heart.

So the question remains: why does God allow bad things to happen? No one can argue that evil does not exist in our world. Jesus promises that we will face trials. Pain and suffering are very real in our world and in our lives. Ignoring that reality does not strengthen our faith; it weakens it. But in Jesus, we can find peace and confidence in the midst of our tribulation, not because it is explained, but because He is present. So if we know that trials and tribulations stand in our past, present, and future, what do we need to know about them that can help frame our mindset?

Before I point us to some difficult passages, let me share where I've personally landed.

As a sinner, what I deserve is death and separation from God. That is what my actions deserve. I have made many mistakes knowingly and willingly. Those wrongdoings should separate me from a perfect and holy God. Instead, the wrath that I deserved was placed on Jesus Christ as the payment for my sins. A payment that I could not make but should have been forced to. With this groundwork laid, it's hard for me to say that "I deserve a happy, easy life." We just established what I truly deserve. So, here's the part that I've come to accept. Anything beyond that is more than I deserve. My experience with Noah was devastating, but I don't deserve an experience with him at all. I was blessed with the opportunity to know him and will be blessed with the time to spend eternity alongside him. I far too often fall into the trap of minimizing my sin and maximizing my efforts. Yet, my self-righteousness is like filthy rags.

The perspective shift for me is an appropriate view of what I deserve. From this place, I am able to wrestle with this question.

Below are several verses that I returned to often.

"My brethren, count it all joy when you fall into various trials, knowing that the testing of your faith produces patience. But let patience have its perfect work, that you may be perfect and complete, lacking nothing."

James 1:2-4 NKJV

"And not only that, but we also glory in tribulations, knowing that tribulation produces perseverance; and perseverance, character; and character, hope. Now hope does not disappoint, because the love of God has been poured out in our hearts by the Holy Spirit who was given to us."

Romans 5:3-5 NKJV

"Though He was a Son, yet He learned obedience by the things which He suffered."

Hebrews 5:8 NKJV

"Furthermore, we have had human fathers who corrected us, and we paid them respect. Shall we not much more readily be in subjection to the Father of spirits and live? For they indeed, for a few days chastened us as seemed best to them, but He, for our profit, that we may be partakers of His holiness. Now no chastening seems to be joyful for the present, but painful; nevertheless, afterward it yields the peaceable fruit of righteousness to those who have been trained by it."

Hebrews 12:9-11 NKJV

"For godly sorrow produces repentance leading to salvation, not to be regretted; but the sorrow of the world produces death."

2 Corinthians 7:10 NKJV

There are many ways to try and tackle this very, very intense question, *"Why does God allow bad things to happen?"* CS Lewis wrote a very insightful book called The Problem of Pain. There are many books and articles available that have tried to tackle this question. We first have to acknowledge again that God's ways are higher than our ways and His thoughts are higher than our thoughts. From that place, here's one of the approaches that we can take when trying to reason an answer.

Genesis 1:31 says that God looked out over all of creation and said that it was very good. You have Adam and Eve walking in the garden with God, perfect walking amidst perfection, with the tree of life and the tree of the knowledge of good and evil. One tree they were told not to eat of (the tree of knowledge of good and evil), the other they were given a chance to eat of (the tree of life). They chose to disobey God and eat of the tree of the knowledge of good and evil. Sin is rebelling against God's law and making our own.

And out of perfection came the curse, often called the fall by many Christian denominations. So what does this mean? Why was this allowed to happen? If life in the garden of Eden was perfect, why did God allow Adam and Eve to "fall" away from Him?

When asked what the greatest commandments were, Jesus said to love God and then to love others. A foundation for love is the freedom to choose. Without the freedom to choose, our relationship is not one of love but of slavery. Part of the mystery of the Gospel is how the power of the sovereignty of God is not hindered in the free choice of His creation.

So sin enters the perfect creation. It has been said that there are two forms of evil, moral and natural. As we wrestled with why a good God allows such abnormalities, we had to categorize the brokenness we saw:

- *Moral Evil: The wrongdoing and rebellion born from our own free will.*

- *Natural Evil: The disasters, sickness, and death caused by the curse of a broken world.*

Noah's diagnosis was natural evil, but God's response was supernatural presence.

We see this spelled out in Genesis 3 and then played out from Genesis 4 through Revelation 21.

So we can continue to wrestle with the why, and that's okay. It's okay to ask questions of God, but we must be willing to accept that He won't always answer.

But if allowing an opportunity for love through choice gives the possibility of rejection, sin, and suffering, how are we to live out our lives? How are we to take heart?

God has not explained Himself to us in the way we once wanted. What He has done is remain faithful, present, and near. Trust, we are learning, is not built on understanding everything God allows, but on believing who He has shown Himself to be, even when the answers don't come on this side of Heaven.

THE ARK: Faith rests on God's character, not on
resolved explanations.

CHAPTER 20

LIVING WITH THE QUESTION

Following the example of David.

On September 17th, 2019, we were told that our son had abnormalities on his ultrasound. That hit our family like a tidal wave. It proceeded into testing, more doctor's visits, and more ultrasounds, which confirmed our fears. Our son, Noah Clifton Efird, had been diagnosed with Trisomy 13. Eventually, I fell back on the only story that made sense to me, David.

2 Samuel 12 tells the story of David's adulterous relationship with Bathsheba and how he had sinned against God. While not a picture-perfect example for us to cling to, his interaction with the sickness and then the death of his son is where we focused.

"David pleaded with God for the boy. He fasted and went into his house and spent the night lying in sackcloth on the ground."

2 Samuel 12:16 NKJV

"He is dead," they replied. Then David got up from the ground, washed and anointed himself, changed his clothes, and went into the house of the LORD and worshiped. Then he went to his own house, and at his request they set food before him, and he ate. "What is this you have done?" his servants asked. "While the child was alive, you fasted and wept, but when he died, you got up and ate." David answered, "While the child was alive, I fasted and wept, for I said, 'Who knows? The LORD may be gracious to me and let him live.' But now that he is dead, why should I fast? Can I bring him back again? I will go to him, but he will not return to me."

2 Samuel 12:19b-23 NKJV

As a family, we began fasting, praying, and weeping for God to save our son. We were confident that God would heal our son, either this side of eternity or the next, but we would sit and wait. And when he was healed, we would commit to rising and worshiping, knowing that we would one day soon be reunited with our son.

Another passage that we spoke over our family very frequently was Psalm 23, which you may be familiar with.

"The Lord is my shepherd; I shall not want. He makes me to lie down in green pastures; He leads me beside the still waters. He restores my soul; He leads me in the paths of righteousness. For His name's sake. Yea, though I walk

through the valley of the shadow of death, I will fear no evil;
For You are with me; Your rod and Your staff, they comfort
me. You prepare a table before me in the presence of my
enemies; You anoint my head with oil; My cup runs over.
Surely goodness and mercy shall follow me all the days of my
life; And I will dwell in the house of the Lord Forever."

Psalm 23 NKJV

We go to scripture, knowing that He will turn our mourning into dancing. Knowing that Noah was fearfully and wonderfully made, from Psalm 139:14. Knowing that we will one day see our son again. Jehovah Rapha, the God who heals. Yet, we hurt. We struggle. We weep. And that's okay. The church as a whole struggles with grief because it cannot be programmed or planned. It's difficult. It's hard. But it doesn't need to be pushed aside. Grief becomes harmful when it's overlooked or avoided. When it's heavily medicated or never spoken of, grief is all-consuming. We need to engage with people in their grief. We need to be present for them over and over again. We need to ask questions. We can help people mourn by creating spaces for them to ask difficult questions. Remember, Grief keeps you at the grave. Mourning moves you forward.

THE ARK: Faith is faithful before and after the outcome.

THE TABLE GOD PREPARES

An invitation to sit in the presence of your enemies.

> *C. S. Lewis said, "God whispers to us in our pleasure. He speaks to us in our conscience. But He shouts to us in our pain. Pain is God's megaphone to rouse a deaf world."*

God had been screaming in our lives. He had us in the valley of the shadow of death. And yet, in the presence of our enemy, a lethal diagnosis for our son, God prepared this beautiful table. Our enemy was hungry to steal our hope. But this table was prepared by a Savior whose hands had already bled, and He would be the one with the final word. He built a table with many seats. I've always found it interesting that it's not a chair.

What we learned is that our grief isn't just for us. We've said it often, this is not the story we wanted, but it's the story we've been given. A story has power and purpose when it's shared and told, not put on a shelf to collect dust. The collective church has often done a poor job of allowing people to suffer. It's as if we've put blinders on, rendering us unable to experience our own suffering or see the suffering in the world around us, even though we know suffering is part of our story. If we don't engage with our own suffering, it won't produce the qualities we aspire to.

While we don't seek out suffering, we embrace it when it comes, taking one day at a time, as our Savior leads us through our suffering. Christianity is unique in that God sent Himself, in the person of Jesus Christ, not to eradicate our suffering but to experience it. To live in it and to provide a path through it. If we allow ourselves to process pain and suffering rather than run from them, seats will open up at our table. You can use your pain as a rod to beat others with or as an open hand to serve them. If we choose the latter, we will see the seats at our table as an opportunity for others to come and experience the goodness and mercy of God in the midst of their trial. We will point them to the One who provides hope and confidence.

We are hurting, but we aren't hopeless. Our wounds are very fresh and very raw, but we trust in our Savior. We serve a Savior who gave us the chance for a relationship. We serve a Savior who provides redemption through His presence in our suffering. Surely goodness and mercy are pursuing me all the days of my life.

With Jesus, our pain creates seats at our table for goodness and mercy.

It's okay that you are struggling. It's okay that you are wrestling. It's okay that you are longing. The only place that you will find peace and confidence is in Jesus Christ: He alone. We have to let people not be okay. We have to give them space to not be okay and be there for them as they move toward Jesus. Only Jesus can turn our mourning into dancing.

Jesus never stopped His ministry on the path to suffering. He did not wait for the pain to pass before continuing to love, heal, and serve.

Focusing on a single point in time prevents us from seeing the full story. The full story of the Bible from cover to cover is the story of redemption. The story of our continual rebellion and the ever-present grace and mercy of God being extended to His people, from the clothing of Adam and Eve in the garden to His death, burial, and resurrection, to His return.

He didn't remove suffering from our lives; He entered into it and made an avenue through it.

> *"Do you now believe?" Jesus replied. "A time is coming and in fact has come when you will be scattered, each to your own home. You will leave me all alone. Yet I am not alone, for my Father is with me. I have told you these things so that in me you may have peace. In this world, you will have trouble. But take heart! I have overcome the world."*
>
> *John 16:31-33 NIV*

Jesus stood abandoned so that we wouldn't have to. He says, in my time of need, you will abandon me, but in your time of need, I will never abandon you. Because He stood in our place, we can find peace.

> *Peace isn't the absence of conflict; it is the presence of a Savior.*

Peace doesn't yet remove the pain in our lives. With the presence of sin in our world, we will always have heartache until Jesus returns again. No, peace doesn't yet remove the pain in our lives. The presence of peace provides us with the courage to have confidence that God will redeem our story.

Peace is not a magic eraser. It doesn't just magically remove the pain in our lives.

THE ARK: Peace is finding rest in the confidence of God's redemption.

Jesus would have been trained by Joseph in the family business of carpentry. Carpenters were known for working hard with their hands to mold and shape the materials they were working with. They would do the hard work, the dirty work, the work that the wood couldn't do on its own, to create something beautiful. They would redeem the wood into something beautiful. At the end of the project, they would take off their apron and carefully fold it to lay over the edge of the table or the piece of furniture. This act would signify that the work was complete.

When the disciples ran to see the empty tomb, they found Jesus' grave clothes carefully folded and laid at the head of the bench in which they laid His body.

This finished work of Jesus Christ is why you and I can find peace in the midst of trials. The table God prepares in our suffering is not the end of the story; it's an invitation to sit, stay, and trust Him as He redeems it. The Carpenter doesn't look at the raw, splintered wood of your life and walk away. He isn't afraid of the jagged edges of your grief or the mess of your bad days. He is right there with you, doing the work that you can't do on your own, molding your wailing into a dance that only He can choreograph.

THE ARK: With Jesus, our pain creates seats at our table for goodness and mercy.

CHAPTER 22

THE FOUNDATIONAL ARK

Jesus is the only solid ground for your table.

We have wrestled with the 'why' of suffering and seen the table God prepares in the midst of it. But an invitation to a table requires a firm foundation beneath it. To sit at the table of redemption, you have to know the Carpenter who built it.

Jesus is the only ground on which you can stand to truly navigate your grief. It's okay to not be okay, but it's not okay for us to stay that way. In the presence of our Savior, we find freedom. Not freedom that all of our struggles are magically removed from our lives, but freedom to navigate through the struggles and trials in life.

If we don't come to grips with the reality of suffering in our lives, then when we are met with suffering, we will feel as if God has abandoned us. Death forces us to focus. Focus dictates direction. The direction you and I go must be into the presence of our Savior. Don't feel abandoned in the midst of your chaos. Stop running. He's right there with you.

There is freedom from sin found in the finished work of Jesus Christ. In the presence of our Savior is freedom. The experience of freedom is directly tied to the strength of the liberator. Our liberator, our Savior, Jesus Christ, had the strength to conquer death. He boldly died on a cross, was laid in a tomb, and rose again three days later to provide an avenue for you and me to be in the presence of God. His presence doesn't overlook your present sorrow, your anxiety, your trials, your hurt, your questions. His presence provides a way through them. He is Jehovah Shammah. The Lord is There. When we accept Jesus Christ as our Lord and Savior, He will be right there with us, providing freedom and restoration throughout our lives.

There is a story in the New Testament that I find such hope in. Maybe you've heard it before. Luke 15 talks about the prodigal son. Tim Keller has penned an amazing resource on this popular parable called The Prodigal God. I highly recommend it! If you are not familiar with the parable, Jesus is teaching a crowd of people, divided into two groups: 1) sinners and tax collectors, and 2) the Pharisees and scribes. In our modern terms, a group of "clearly" lost, sinful people and a group of "clearly" saved and good people. Clearly is in quotations because we fall into the trap of judging others far too quickly, when only God truly knows the condition of someone's heart. So to address these two groups of people, Jesus tells a parable about a father who has two sons.

The younger son chooses to leave the family and go off on his own. Not uncommon in our day, but in the audience of Jesus, this was a big deal. When the younger son asked for his portion of the inheritance, he was effectively telling his dad, "Dad, you are dead to me." The father goes to great lengths and sacrifices to divide up all that he owns, and the young man leaves home. His journey takes him into a foreign land, without friends, family, or community, and he lives as many do with a windfall inheritance. He wastes it. Something that has always seemed significant to me is verse 14, that a severe famine takes place in the land where he was. How often do we find ourselves trying to live within our own means and feeling like we are in a barren wasteland? When the alarm goes off, and you can already feel the hangover or the emptiness of coming off the high. When you roll over and don't know the name of the person beside you. When you refuse to look at yourself in the mirror because of the shame that you feel. Barren wasteland. Famine. You are trying to consume all that the world tells you will fill you, but you truly know that you are starving. Empty inside.

The son wanted what he considered total freedom, but this 'freedom' led to his slavery. A lot of times, we misunderstand someone's authority in our lives. Let me demonstrate. How many of you became frustrated when your parents told you not to play in the road? Honestly, think about this, though. I can remember my brother and me being seriously upset when my parents told us. In my small mind, I couldn't understand why they would try to prevent me from having such fun in the road. Thankfully, my parents had the wisdom to foresee that the road was home to these massive objects called cars that moved at 55+mph. I thought, "How selfish of you to keep me from playing in the road. You are putting unnecessary chains on my life, Mom and Dad. I wish you would give me some freedom. I can't even believe y'all." And all the while, my parents are saying,

"Son, if you could only see what we see. Son, if you only knew the certain pain that awaits you if you play in the road. Son, I don't let you because I love you. Son, I want the best for you. Son, you need to trust me. Son, I have your best interest at heart, and it is because I love you so much."

Maybe you find yourself in this season at a loss for words. You look around yourself at the barren wasteland. This moment in time for you can be like that of the younger son. He realizes he has sold himself into slavery to feed pigs. While his spiritual hunger was there, so was his physical hunger. His physical hunger is what God used to wake him up to his surroundings.

"But when he came to himself, he said, 'How many of my father's hired servants have bread enough and to spare, and I perish with hunger! I will arise and go to my father, and will say to him, "Father, I have sinned against heaven and before you, and I am no longer worthy to be called your son. Make me like one of your hired servants."

Luke 15:17-19 NKJV

He thought back to his father's house. He thought back to all of the hired hands and servants. How well they were treated and the amount of food they were given. His father's house wasn't defined by famine. It was defined by a feast. This younger son was fine to call himself a hired hand or a servant, but he had to escape this famine. But how do you return to the man that you told was dead to you? The son develops a plan to go home with a 3-point speech. First, he would say, "I have sinned against heaven and in your sight." Second, he would say, "I am no longer worthy to be called your son." Third, he would say, "Make me like one of your hired servants". He is admitting his failing, his separation, and offering his solution to make it better.

I imagine this young man, covered in filth, on his knees in the pigpen as his body aches from the pains originating in his stomach. He looks up out of the mess towards home. He rehearses his speech one more time, then he stands up. He starts walking towards home. Imagine this broken son walking past the house that had been enslaving him for so long. Imagine him walking past the town where he had blown all his possessions. Maybe he saw people that he had thought were his friends. Maybe he saw girls that he thought were going to satisfy him. Maybe he saw taverns that he thought were going to quench his thirst. But as he got outside of the town, he still had a long way to walk. Imagine walking this road, this bumpy road, full of rocks and roots, things that could trip him up. Imagine him passing people who are going back to that town. Maybe for an instant, he thought, I should go back. It's better to go back. But then he thinks back to the pig sty, and he begins to rehearse his lines for his father.

As he walks, he rehearses "I have sinned against heaven and in your sight. I am no longer worthy to be called your son. Make me like one of your hired servants." Over and over, step after step, as he returns home. Finally, the landscape starts to look familiar. As he gets closer, the pain coming up from his stomach is covered by the anxiety of how his father will respond. Step by step, he gets closer. He begins to anticipate seeing his old house over the horizon. He begins to recite his pitch faster and faster. Maybe his heart races a little bit, then he tops the hill, and he sees the house. The house that he probably grew up in. I imagine him being completely overwhelmed with emotions. Then he takes a deep breath and keeps walking.

Then we get reintroduced to the father in this parable. What is his response to this son who has abandoned the family? He is actively seeking for his son to return. He is looking. I imagine the father each night looking out over the horizon, scanning, hoping that his son will come home. Each morning, the first thing he does when he gets up is look over that horizon. He watches the sun rise in the East and hopes to see his son's shadow coming across the hillside. Then at night, he watches as the sun sets, hoping that it will hold out just long enough to provide his son enough light to get home. I imagine that he would check often throughout the day.

The younger son was still a far way off, yet the father saw him. The father instantly had compassion on him. The word Jesus used here for compassion is that his heart was overwhelmed, or literally "to have the bowels yearn." At this time in Biblical history, mankind believed that the bowels were the seat of love and pity. A more accurate image however, is a gut-wrenching compassion, similar to the gut-wrenching pain felt by the younger son. Not too far off from the gut-wrenching pain the younger son has been feeling. It's not like, awe, that's cute. It's that overwhelming emotion that starts in your gut and spurs out of you. What did the overwhelming compassion lead the father to do?

The father ran to his son. Men did not run during this time period. In the first century, however, a Middle Eastern man never — never — ran. If he were to run, he would have to pick up his tunic, his outer robe, so he would not trip. If he lifted his tunic, his bare legs would be visible, which would be a humiliating and shameful act for a man in that culture. What an example of love!

But the son isn't guaranteed that this is an act of love. Can you imagine with me the son seeing his father running towards him? Should he curl up into the fetal position? Should he run away? Should he be ready to fight? Then it happens. The father throws his arms around his son and kisses him. Can you even imagine the stench that was on this son? Can you even imagine the amount of pig filth that he was covered in? I imagine that he had probably lost a lot of weight. His face may have been mangled from fights he got in. Yet even in all the mess that surrounded him, the father embraces him and kisses him. A kiss is such an intimate display of emotions. The father wraps his son up and kisses him.

The son, confused and overwhelmed, starts into his well-rehearsed pitch, but something miraculous happens.

> *"And the son said to him, 'Father, I have sinned against heaven and in your sight, and am no longer worthy to be called your son.'*
>
> *"But the father said to his servants, 'Bring out the best robe and put it on him, and put a ring on his hand and sandals on his feet. And bring the fatted calf here and kill it, and let us eat and be merry; for this my son was dead and is alive again; he was lost and is found.' And they began to be merry."*
>
> *Luke 15:21–24 NKJV*

See what happened? Go back and read it again. I'll wait.

The son doesn't complete his pitch. A great sales pitch presents a problem and then solves it in a very short timeframe. The son isn't able to solve the problem here. He is able to admit his failing and his separation, but not offer his solution.

Can I bring this home for you and me? This is how Jesus meets us. Covered in the filth of our sin and rebellion. We are met with such grace. We acknowledge our failing and our separation, then Jesus provides the solution.

In the parable, the younger son is given a robe, a ring, and a pair of sandals.

The best robe would have been one of the Father's robes. Even though the son was filthy (he had been in the pig sty, something that was detestable to the Jewish culture), the Father embraced him and then clothed him with the finest robe - His own.

> *"For He made Him who knew no sin to be sin for us, that we might become the righteousness of God in Him."*
>
> *2 Corinthians 5:21 NKJV*

Through the finished work of Jesus Christ, we are clothed in righteousness.

A ring at this time was the sign of the family. It was like a family crest. It was used to seal letters that were sent out, especially those of prominence. From the text, we can infer that this man was fairly wealthy, so his ring was something that stated whose family he belonged to. The Father wanted to show very clearly that the son was part of the family. Also, the idea was that a ring's seal would keep letters safe until the proper time to open them, and that everyone who saw the letter would know who it came from/who owned it.

> *"In Him you also trusted, after you heard the word of truth, the gospel of your salvation; in whom also, having believed, you were sealed with the Holy Spirit of promise, who is the guarantee of our inheritance until the redemption of the purchased possession, to the praise of His glory."*
>
> *Ephesians 1:13-14 NKJV*

By the Holy Spirit, we are marked and sealed for eternity through the finished work of Jesus Christ on the cross.

A pair of sandals. How practical are a pair of sandals? In this culture, they walked everywhere. Sandals were crucial. If the son had literally lost everything, that probably includes his sandals. The Father gave him something practical for the rest of his journey. Ephesians tells us to prepare our feet with the Gospel of Peace. I think that is our practical implementation here. Our Heavenly Father gives us eternal peace by knowing as a Christian where our Salvation lies and Whose hands it lies in. Because of that, we are given peace.

Do you know who didn't have sandals? Slaves. You know who did have sandals? Sons!

As a Christian, our identity has been forever changed.

My ultimate prayer for you is that you will accept this free gift. It's as easy as the ABCs. Admit you are a sinner in need of a Savior. Believe that Jesus Christ came, lived the perfect life, died the death that you and I deserve, and rose three days later, having conquered death. Confess Him as Lord over your life and commit to follow Him.

THE ARK: Jesus is the only ground on which you can stand to truly navigate your grief.

CHAPTER 23

AVOID THE VOID

Smoothing the sharp internal edges of loss.

Our fear is feeling. Don't avoid the void. If you find yourself numb from the grief, my heart breaks for you. I've been there. There were days that I didn't know if I would ever feel again. Here's what I know. Avoiding doesn't bring healing.

I had this void in my heart. It was like a broken window. Sharp edges everywhere. Every attempt to look through it came with a cost. Anytime I allowed my mind to linger on my circumstances, I was met with pain and agony. The temptation was to avoid this void. We both know that would be easier.

Over time, though, by allowing myself to go back to these moments, to remember his life, to remember his death, the edges of the void slowly smoothed out. Did it remove the void? No, it did not. I still have a Noah-sized hole in my heart. I just don't get cut open every time I think about him.

Are there still days when I find a sharp edge? Of course. But now I know that edge needs time. So, I slide up to the edge, allow my heart to hang over the void, and remember my precious son.

For me, talking about him and writing have been deeply healing. Intentionally and painfully walking through every aspect of the story. If you find any hope in my story, I pray that you will do the same with yours. There is healing to be found in our grief, if we are willing to face it.

Avoiding the void may feel safer in the moment, but only by entering it can we begin to heal. Today, find someone who loves you and have them commit to sitting with you once a week through your grief journey. Their only commitment is to show up and ask some questions.

You can send them this text: "Hey friend. I really could use your help. Would you be willing to sit with me for a coffee once a week? I want someone to walk with me through this."

If you are that loved one reading this book, invite them to coffee this week. Ask them some questions, listen, and invite them back again next week. I wanted to be asked questions about our family, about the pregnancy, about work, about my favorite football team, about how I was feeling, and about how they could pray for me.

Facing the void is a lonely work, but it was never meant to be a solo mission. While you are busy trying to find your footing and smooth out those sharp internal edges, you are going to need to lean on the people God has placed around you. Sometimes, survival requires borrowing strength from others until your own returns.

THE ARK: Healing begins where avoidance ends.

THE COMMUNITY MANUAL

For the People Who Love Someone in the Waves

These chapters are not just for the griever. They are for you: the friend, the family member, the person who wants to help and does not know how.

What follows is a map drawn by people who needed others to show up and experienced firsthand what it looked like when they did and when they didn't.

Read it. Then go love your person.

CHAPTER 24

BORROWED STRENGTH

*Letting others hold the line when
you can't stand.*

We leaned heavily on our community once we found out about Noah's diagnosis.

Don't steal someone's blessing by not accepting help. Our family finds so much joy in helping others. We have been deeply blessed, and this was the first season where we found ourselves in desperate need. We were told early on to let others help so as not steal their blessing. So many people within our sweet community hurt deeply with us, and like us, there was nothing they could do to "fix it". Allowing people to cook meals, watch our oldest son for a date night, or send care packages (where we got the original idea for Noah's Arks in Even

Though, We Will). We were able to lean on our community for help; this was crucial for our grieving family. Little did we know that it would only get more difficult, and we would lean harder on family and dear friends. Going to the grocery store was enough mental and physical energy for the day. So many doctors' appointments and meetings, free childcare was a huge blessing!

If you know someone who has been flung into this season, send them food. If they have kids, pay for or be the babysitter so they can go on a drive or out to dinner. No, really, send them food or pay for a babysitter, or do both! These are tangible ways that you can love and support them. It's not a "least you can do." It really makes an impact.

At the onset of grief, words are not needed. Don't try to rush them. Your presence is all they need. Don't try to fill their void. Simple tasks are a welcome breath of fresh air. Cut the grass, wash the cars, offer to do loads of laundry, or bring them dinner. During our initial season of hurting, we had let a few friends into it to have a seat at our table. These friends would bring dinner and not be offended if we sent them away, but kept the food. We only have the strength to tell you to 'send the food' because we know the life-giving power of a meal that was prepared by someone else's hands when ours were too heavy to move.

THE ARK: Letting others help is an act of grace, for them and for you.

CHAPTER 25

HURTING, HEALING, HELPING

A map for the spectrum of grief.

Borrowing strength is a vital part of the process, but eventually, you need a map to understand where all that strength is going. For our family, that map took the form of three distinct but overlapping seasons: Hurting, Healing, and Helping. Finding 'health' meant learning how to navigate each one without trying to rush the clock.

The goal here is health. See the Venn diagram of hurting, healing, and helping. At the center of these three, we find health. In the presence of grief, we must acknowledge that each of these will be part of our story moving forward.

We found different seasons in our grief that ebbed and flowed through. Like a rainbow, you can see distinct colors from afar, but up close, they blend into a single spectrum of light. There is a blending of the spectrum of grief and pain that I didn't anticipate. I like to accomplish a task and move on; I'm not a 'circle back' kind of guy. Noah taught me that life ebbs and flows, like the rising and falling of the tides. His life forced me to examine my own life and my ability to process. When we were hit with Abnormalities, we were thrown headlong into a deep season of hurting.

Hurting: the one no one sees coming. Our initial season of hurting held a lot of tears, a lot of questions, a lot of restless nights, and a lot of numbness and fatigue. It felt as if we were shells of our previous selves. I was there physically, but emotionally and mentally, it was this thick cloud of confusing fog. Mentally, we were exhausted. Normal, everyday tasks became difficult to accomplish, and I became very forgetful. Thankfully, I had trained myself to use my calendar in our businesses, so I defaulted to my highest level of training and put everything into my calendar as it came up, because if I didn't, almost 100% of the time I would forget about it. Emotionally, we were frail and fragile. Certain songs, phrases, or scenes in a movie would wreck you. Walker's learning to process his emotions as a two-year-old created a unique experience for our family in that we all learned/relearned together how to feel and how to communicate how we were feeling.

Trying to define this season is like trying to catch the wind. You can see it and the effects that it has on those around it, but knowing exactly when, where, and how hard it will blow is outside of your realm of possibility. You also know areas that typically have more force. My parents have windchimes set up on their back porch because the breeze blows through, and it makes a beautiful sound. The more time you spend in a place, the more you understand its patterns. A pattern of intensely focused hurting was writing our story down. Reliving the events of Noah's life forced me to walk headlong into the storm.

Our season of hurting was unique in that we were given a diagnosis of grief that was yet to come. So in our grief, we had three seasons of grieving during Noah's pregnancy, grieving with Noah in person at the hospital, and now living in grief with Noah in Heaven.

FEEL, NOT FILL

If I can implore you, please feel, don't fill. Filling will not allow you to get to healing. When a patient has a puncture wound, the paramedics pack the wound to get it to stop bleeding, but they don't leave it packed with gauze and send you home, hoping you get better. You are seen by a skilled surgeon who removes the gauze, examines the wound, and then goes about repairing what has been torn and cut beneath the surface. When they are finished, they will be able to sew up the surface and allow the body to heal. In this scenario, even the most skilled surgeons leave some kind of mark on the skin. While you may be healing, you will always be marked by this void. It will never be filled, even when it is healed. God, in His mercy, is the one who can bring healing into the deepest part of your void, but He won't replace it. While He is always enough, He doesn't remove it from your life. God's redemption is not about removing; it's about healing. Redemption is the payment of ransom for one in bondage and slavery. It doesn't remove the fact that you were in bondage and slavery, but it provides a path for you to walk in the newness of life hand in hand with your Savior, Jesus Christ. Noah's life has forever marked our family. We will always miss him until we are with him again in Heaven. We will always hurt from the void in our lives, but there is a healing filled with grace and mercy from our Heavenly Father. It is found in intentional rest, raw worship, candid prayer, and focused communication.

Healing, the one that everyone longs for and often rushes. I can vividly remember, as a rising Senior in high school, talking with my physical therapist about my recent knee surgery to repair my ACL, MCL, and meniscus from a football injury. She told me, in effect, "Matthew, if you don't take this part seriously, it will not work. This part is hard, and no one likes it. It takes time. It will hurt, and you will be frustrated. You will not feel like yourself for a long time, but you will get better. I will be here to help you, and we will adapt to how your body responds. I must caution you, if you don't take this part seriously by trying to rush it, you will be back here again after your second surgery to fix a new tear. Your body is not designed to perform at a high level with this much damage in it. We must take the time to let the damage heal, let your body be restrengthened around it, and we will get you back onto that field. While your knee will be forever marked from the surgery, if you give it focused time, it will heal, not so that it never happened, but so that you can still play football." Little did I know that, as an eighteen-year-old, how profound this would be for me 10 years later.

Because we have such a tendency to avoid pain, as soon as we can get our feet underneath us in hurting, we run as fast as we can from it, through healing, and try to park ourselves in helping. While avoiding the void may provide some temporary reprieve, it will not provide healing.

AVOID THE VOID. If I can implore you, please do not avoid the void.

Helping: the one where the battle wounds are displayed.

Empathy is a tool, not a weapon.

I can remember a time being at the beach with a storm coming towards that part of the state. It wasn't as big as a tropical storm, but it was enough to create some of the biggest waves we had ever played in. I remember my Dad reminding my brother, Michael, and me that if you get caught in an undertow, swim parallel to the beach, don't try to swim against the current. We played and body surfed, and boogie boarded the waves for what felt like hours. A small resemblance of an undertow would pop up, and we would swim right or left out of it and walk to shore. We had a blast! The storm came in, we went inside, and then we went out to play afterwards. More people were on the beach this time, and I can remember standing in almost chest-deep water waiting for the next wave when all of a sudden, the water color quickly changed around me, and I felt something hit me in the back.

I turned around, and it was a little boy with his swimmies on. He and I were now in the midst of a strong undertow. I picked him up out of the water and asked if he was okay. After assuring me that he could swim back to shore, I placed him down in front of me towards the beach, so that I stood between him and the depth of the sea. Immediately, he slid into me. It was all that I could do just to stand, much less swim directly into the current. All of my years of training to hold the line while playing football were coming into play. Because of my experience in the undertow and my strength forged in years of training and battles on the football field, I carried this little boy diagonally to shore, where his dad was sprinting into the water to hug him and me. All of this happened in less than a minute, but I was in the right place at the right time with the right experiences. I was able to react in such a way that this little boy, being dragged out to sea, was carried safely to shore. That's how helping works. Helping is engaging with the redemption of your pain, your loss, your grief, for the glory of God and the benefit of others, all the while continuing to strengthen the healing of your own void.

The dark side of empathy is knowing how to help and choosing to watch someone else suffer. If we choose to just sit on the sidelines, we will miss out on part of our healing. There is a part of the depth of our grieving soul that needs to engage with the side of helping to fully experience health in this area. But there is a deeper part to this darkness. When you are caught between Hurting and Healing, the dark side of empathy is the voice that tells you no one truly understands, so you shouldn't even try to let them in. It's the temptation to weaponize your pain, to look at the 'normal' lives of those around you and judge them for their lack of scars. If we stay there, empathy becomes a wall instead of a bridge.

In your journey, you will eventually reach a crossroads: you can either let bitterness and self-pity consume you, or you can allow God to heal the void in your heart. As much as I would like to tie a pretty bow on these seasons and encourage you that you will be in Hurting for 3 months and healing for 1 year and helping for the rest of your life, that's not how grief works. I pray that I have earned enough respect with you at this point in our story to speak candidly into your life and into the depth of your hurting heart. There is no pretty bow that will ever be tied onto your grief. We were reminded at Noah's memorial service that this part of our family would be forever gone, never to be filled. Not lost, as we believe we will see him again one day, but missing in our present reality.

The roughness of the edges would smooth with time, but the hole would remain. As I examine my heart, I can almost seem to run my fingers across that void. I can sense its depth. I can feel its sting. I can also appreciate the time spent there, slowly smoothing some of the edges as I've sat down to stay a while many times since that first doctor's appointment. We fear pain and suffering such that we avoid them, rather than allowing ourselves to experience, process, and be marked by them.

In my reading during this journey, I came across the words of another grieving father struggling to put words to his heart's ache from the passing of his son. "If he was worth loving, he is worth grieving. Grief is existential testimony to the worth of the one loved. That worth abides. So I own my grief. I do not try to put it behind me, to get over it, to forget it...It belongs within my story. Every lament is a love song." If you allow Him, God will redeem your grief in each season for His glory, but it will always hurt. Noah was worth loving, and he is worth grieving. The same goes for you. If they were worth loving, they are worth grieving.

The presence of hurting does not negate the presence of healing. Allowing yourself time to heal does not mean that you are unequipped for times of helping. Your ability to help others does not mean that you still have room for healing. You can be healing and still hurting at the same time. You can be helping and still healing in the very same moments. You can and will ebb and flow between each season, not as finished works but as rest stops. Some days you will rest in one area longer than others.

Hurting, healing, and helping are not destinations: they are places we rest along the way. We return to them as needed, not because we are failing, but because grief is carried, not completed.

THE ARK: Health comes from honoring every season, not skipping them.

EMPATHY: A TOOL I DIDN'T WANT

*Learning to listen to understand,
not to respond.*

I didn't want empathy; I wanted my son back. But through the beautiful exhaustion of sharing our story over and over, I realized that the people who helped me the most weren't the ones who spoke the best theology; they were the ones who were willing to be exhausted with me. They didn't come to fix; they came to hear.

Empathy is a tool that I didn't want. It is also something that I hear thrown around with little thought as to what it truly is and the potential power it holds. Empathy is a tool that can quickly be misused for selfish purposes. I can remember the sting of the words "I know exactly what you are going through"... The first few times I heard this, I was really upset at the naivety and selfishness of the people around me, but then I became saddened by their own unawareness. Empathy shouldn't be about turning the story and focusing on you. We love to talk about ourselves, but in the moments that empathy is needed, that is the last thing that is helpful. The easier path is to turn the focus on yourself and avoid the void in your life. For the sake of the person hurting in your life, don't take the easy path. Resist the temptation to talk about yourself. Be someone in their life displaying true Empathy.

Empathy is the ability to identify and relate with someone else's emotions created from a similar experience. Notice my definition is very intentionally written as such. Empathy is an ability, something that can be improved upon by your own self-awareness and your willingness to listen. Like listening, empathy is something that some naturally excel in, while others struggle greatly. My hope is that you and I will learn to be more empathetic with those in our lives. Empathy causes us to turn the focus onto someone else in our pursuit of identifying and relating to the emotions this person is having. Engaging with someone with empathy is not the time to assume that you know everything about them. When we first found out about Noah's diagnosis, I had someone with good intentions say, "I know you are so mad, and if you just need to scream at God, you can always call me, and I'll listen." Did you catch it? Beyond trying to be God, they tried to define my emotions for me without even having discussed it with me. They used their similar experience and transposed their emotions onto me. Their attempt at helping was actually hurting, giving me a confusing, false sense of my own emotions.

My confusion came in that I wasn't mad. I wasn't angry. In the eyes of this individual, I had every 'right' to be angry, and yet I wasn't. While I have struggled with expressing the emotion of anger throughout my life, in this season, I was not bubbling up with anger. I was experiencing overwhelming sadness. It was like the color in my life had been sucked out by a vacuum. My life wasn't tinted with red as this person had assumed; it was shaded in grey and filled with ache. We had several people who handled this very well. They navigated our grief with compassionate questions and their presence. They proactively sought to identify the emotions we were experiencing and examine their life in order to find ways to relate.

When people seeking to engage with empathy would hear our story, their demeanor would change. The tension in their body would release. The angst in their face would drop. They would slow down and focus, looking us in the eyes. Oftentimes, they would place a hand on our shoulder or our knee. They would wade out into the waters with us, seeking to truly hear us. When we met someone like this, our hearts would overflow with emotion. We would share our fears, our hurts, our confusion, and they would do this magical thing called listening. Here's a piece of advice that I have learned. Empathy requires listening to understand, not listening to respond. They have very different styles of listening.

Remember, our requirements for empathy are to identify and relate. You can never be truly empathetic if you aren't willing to stop and listen. When you listen well, you get to hear their story, exposing you to the causes of their emotions. While they may not see the correlation yet, you are also serving as a conduit for their healing process. We cannot avoid the void, or it will never heal. By talking about it to a truly listening ear, we are slowly smoothing out the edges. By listening well, you are using empathy as a tool to help this person in your life walk through the healing process.

As you listen, you will hear similarities in your experiences. Remember, listen with the intent to understand, not to respond. As you understand, you can offer things that helped you navigate the emotions, but please know that listening is enough. There are plenty of people out there who will talk a lot, but rarely will someone just listen. If you find yourself thrown into the seas of grief, you will welcome the tender comfort of a listening ear with open arms. Be that rare place of safety for those hurting in your life. In the midst of that safety, you can share your story.

There is a major difference between the theoretical and the experienced in the midst of grief. I don't want to hear what you think might be a good way to navigate hurt. I want to know how you survived when you were thrown against the wall. When tragedy struck, how did you get out of bed? How did you continue to talk with your spouse in a loving way? How did you go back to work? Share with me things that worked for you in the midst of your grief, not as a way to fix and remove my pain, but as a resource to help me survive the storm of hurting. The old adage holds so true in the midst of grief: People don't care how much you know until they know how much you care. If you've taken the time to actively listen to my story, I am much more likely to receive your input rather than to be defensive of it. The epicenter of our hurt was the diagnosis that our son had received and the journey that we would be on through the pregnancy and delivery at the hospital, only to not go home with him.

Trying to speak over my pain was to speak over my son. We would already have so few memories, so few moments, so little time to honor and protect what his life meant to us. To speak too quickly, to define our emotions for us, or to rush us toward resolution felt like another loss layered on top of the first. Noah's life deserved to be handled with care, and so did our grief.

True empathy does not rush to fill the silence, define the emotions, or correct the theology. It recognizes that something sacred has been broken and approaches with care. Empathy does not demand access; it waits to be invited. It does not assume authority; it offers availability.

When someone entrusts you with their grief, they are placing something fragile in your hands. How you listen matters. How quickly you speak matters. Whether you try to fix or simply sit matters. Empathy is not about having the right words; it is about creating a safe place for the right words to emerge in time.

If you love someone who is grieving, don't try to rescue them from the pain. Walk with them through it. Listen long enough to learn their story. Honor the story before offering your own. Empathy, when practiced well, becomes a bridge, not out of grief, but through it.

Walking that bridge is exhausting though. It requires you to leave the safety of your own life and step back into the grey with me. When you listen without trying to fix, you are essentially saying, 'I'm willing to be as tired and sad as you are for the next thirty minutes.' It's a beautiful exhaustion. Most people will try to pull you out of the water because they don't like getting wet. But the person who truly helps is the one who jumps in and just treads water beside you until you have the strength to swim again.

Healing often begins the moment someone feels truly heard.

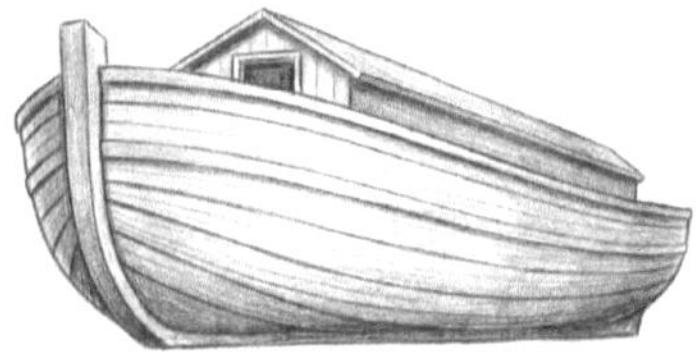

THE ARK: True empathy honors someone's pain by listening before speaking.

CHAPTER 27

QUESTIONS TO AVOID

*Tangible love in action for the
griever and the friend.*

We have experienced that our culture does not allow us to grieve. We were given very profound insight by Deandra right after our diagnosis, sitting around our table. We were talking about coming back to church after having found out. She said, "People will handle this in different ways because they don't know what to say. Some people will avoid you because they don't know what to say. Some people will give you a hug and then move away because they don't know what to say. And some people will say really dumb things because they don't know what to say." We have received many well-intentioned comments and questions that were not helpful in our grieving process. I wanted to share them with you in hopes that you will avoid them.

Don't try to explain away my pain.

1. **Saying: I know exactly what you are going through**

    a. Better: With the pain I have experienced in my life, I cannot imagine what you are going through. I am here for you if you would like to talk. OR I have experienced the pain of loss in my life, and I am so sorry you are walking through this. I am praying for you and am here for you if you'd like to talk.

    b. Why: Empathy can be a really powerful tool when used to connect with someone in the midst of their pain, as we have discussed in previous chapters. Empathy can also be an attempt to turn the attention to yourself rather than allowing the person grieving to connect with their pain. Even identical twins have different stories. Everyone's story is unique to them. While we have similar experiences, assuming that you fully understand what someone else is going through is a very shaky position. If you really want to engage with someone in their grief, use your story as an opportunity to share how you processed/are processing the pain in your life, without assuming that you know everything. Grieving people connect and process on their own timeframe. Allow them to ask you about your story if/when they want to.

    c. Someone handled this so tenderly with me. She shared that she had lost her daughter several years ago, and she had Trisomy 13. She said that she is willing to talk and answer questions about her experience if we ever want to discuss. She gave us her phone number and email and said she would be praying for us.

i.   This approach gave us the freedom to connect with her on our own timeframe.

ii.   She also didn't take her experience and beat us over the head with it. Hurting people don't need additional hurt heaped on them.

2.   **Saying: How are you doing?**

a.   Better: How can I pray for you? Or What is something that your family needs this week?

i.   Pray for rest, mercy, and tenderness in relationships, patience with children, and other ignorant people.

b.   Why: Most days, we aren't doing well. We've shared the analogy of standing in the break of the waves. The thing about standing there is that the waves keep coming. Grief is painful and hard to walk through. Getting asked multiple times a day how you are doing can feel like another wave is hitting. The fact that you see me standing should be enough. We hurt. We cry. We also laugh. I have to confront my situation on a constant basis; don't make me talk about it every time I see you. I know you care.

3.   **Saying: You look like you aren't doing well**

a.   Better: Is there a task this week that I can do for you? Can I run an errand or watch your children for the afternoon?

b.   Why: I wanted to say to these people, "Of course I don't look great! How am I supposed to look?" You may mean that the person you care about is not looking up to their normal, cheery self. Grief is not only an emotional and mental battle but also a physical battle. Great of you to notice the toil that your loved one is walking through, but don't try to add to the burden by pointing it out. When you see this on their face, move into some kind of action. Clean the house, bring by or have dinner delivered, pick up the kids, and let them take a nap. Let your concern move you to action, not to comment.

4. **Saying: God just needed him more than we did**

   a. Better: I'm so sorry for what you are going through. Please know that we are praying for you.

   b. Why: I don't need your weak theology that God needed my son. Please avoid this comment and thought process. There are many times when we don't know what to say, and in the midst of grief, you find yourself searching for words more often than not. Do not find these words.

5. **Saying: Don't lose hope, God can heal him.**

   a. Better: I'm praying for you and for healing in your heart and in their life.

   b. Why: I know that God can heal him. I have been begging Him to since I found out. There is a major difference between losing hope and living within the present circumstances that have been revealed.

6. **Practical: Trying to find the right thing to say or do.**

   a. Grief is a lonely place, and finding the "right" thing to do can feel impossible. Whether you are the one walking through the waves or the one standing on the shore, here are practical ways to bridge the gap:

   b. For the Griever: Receiving Grace

      i. Accept the Silence: Allow yourself to just sit with people without the pressure to talk.

    ii. Talk About "Normal" Life: It is healing to talk about things outside of your grief; it reminds you that while your life has changed, it isn't over.

    iii. Take the Space: Let people take your children for the day so you have the freedom to just sit and feel your emotions.

    iv. Delegate the Routine: Accept help with meals on high-stress days, such as doctor's appointments, to lower your daily burden.

c. For the Friend: Tangible Acts of Love

    i. Be a Constant Presence: Don't try to craft the perfect words; simply show up and be willing to sit in silence.

    ii. Handle the Logistics: Move into action without being asked: clean the house, wash the cars, cut the grass, or offer to do loads of laundry.

    iii. Focus on the Household: Drop off food for lunch or dinner, or have it delivered.

    iv. Take their dog for a night or watch their other children.

    v. Bring toys or treats for the siblings who are also navigating the change.

    vi. Send Thoughtful Anchors: Mail letters or curated care packages with items like candles or games.

    vii. Share books, articles, or songs that provided you comfort, letting them know you are praying for them.

d. We found that cooking on doctor's appointment days was very stressful, so several close friends took turns dropping off dinner on those nights specifically.

THE ARK: Grief does not need interpretation;
it needs companionship.

CHAPTER 28

LETTER TO OUR DOCTORS

The medical professionals who walk through these tragedies see death every day, yet they often carry their own silent grief. We found that expressing our gratitude was a way to find redemption in the sterile hallways of the hospital. I share this letter as an example for you, a way to honor the hands that held yours when yours were too weak to move.

Dear Dr,

Words cannot adequately express our gratitude towards you for the compassionate care that you have provided our family. Noah was so loved by many, including you. Thank you for supporting us during our time with Noah and for helping to honor his life. We pray for you regularly as you continue to serve families that find themselves in crushing circumstances such as ours. We are praying for peace, patience, endurance, and wisdom for your days ahead. Noah's name means rest, and we pray that Jesus will give you rest. We are honored that you were part of our son's life and our family's story!

With love,
The Efirds

CHAPTER 29

SAFE HARBOR

Finding Rest in the Promise.

To my Beauty, my Bride, my Best Friend, I will be forever grateful for you as my partner. Tragedy reveals the raw depth of someone's character, and what beauty it has revealed in you. You are kind and compassionate, tender and loving, thoughtful and bighearted, fierce and loyal, smart and creative. Since September 17, 2019, we have been through a lot. A lot of laughs, a lot of travels, a lot of memories, a lot of pain, a lot of tears, but ultimately a lot of us. We look back on this season and appreciate the deeper forging of our relationship with each other, with God, and with our community. I love you with all that is in me. You will be my favorite, forever and always!

To our friends, we have learned more completely the need for and design of true community. We would not be standing today without your love, your support, your encouragement, and your prayers. Thank you for loving our family so well. If we may be so bold, we'd ask that you continue to pray for us. Continue to pray that we honor Noah's life and process his passing. Pray that our family will continue to move forward, not overlooking our other boys. Lastly, pray that we won't try to fill Noah's void with our other children.

To my sweet Noah, I am a better person because of you, and I will be forever grateful for the courage with which you fought to give your mom and me so much time with you. I miss you, I love you, and I look forward to seeing you again.

Every life is precious, and we seek to honor each uniquely made in the image of our Creator. There will never be another Noah Clifton Efird. His 57.5 hours spent on this side of Heaven will be forever cherished and branded into our family. May we be good stewards of the time we have until we meet him again.

Even Though, We Will

With love,
The Efirds

ACKNOWLEDGMENT

Cloud of Witnesses:

Those Who Stood in the Waves

Our community consisted of so many people. We received hundreds of letters, texts, and emails from people around the country (thank you, Christian Healthcare Ministries, CHM). Free childcare for Walker so that we could go to our many doctor's appointments or try to have a date night. Gift cards, care packages, prayer shawls, books. The list goes on and on. We were loved so well by so many. It would take a full book to attempt to express our gratitude to so many who offered so much. True community acts out of love without need for reciprocation. We love you all so much! With that said, we would like to acknowledge a few people who stood in the waves with us and continue to stand close by us.

To our parents, Chris and Kim, Steve and Kathy, we cannot thank you enough for the prayers, the space, and the listening ear. Your tender love for our family was refreshing. Your hurt was unique in that your children were hurting, and your grandson was hurting. Thank you for leaning in and not avoiding the pain. Thank you for being amazing parents and even better grandparents. We, Walker, Abel, Warren, and Noah have been so richly blessed by each of you!

To my brother, Michael, I cannot thank you enough for going above and beyond at work. It is an honor to work with you, and

I will be forever grateful for the time and the space that you gave me during this season. I am inspired by your loyalty. Thank you for giving it so freely to my family.

To Rob and Deandra, your counsel and wisdom were crucial in our navigating this season. From the many nights around the table, sharing stories and tears, to the difficult questions, we thank you for your example of loving discipleship in the midst of trials. You made calls that we didn't want to. You asked questions that we didn't think of. You were there to celebrate Noah as he went to be with Jesus. You offered exactly what we needed, your consistent presence. And to Mrs. D (our boy's name for Deandra), Walker loves you more than you will ever know. Your willingness to watch him with little notice to allow us to make it to an appointment or to just have a hard day was beyond sacrificial love. Our sincerest Thank You!

To Micah and Haley, your generous care packages were thoughtful, helpful, and a sweet moment to look forward to each month. It was also the origin of the idea of Even Though, We Will. You have been our best friends for years. You loved Noah so well.

To my Bride, your beauty and strength in the midst of trials are awe-inspiring. I am forever grateful for you as my partner. Tragedy reveals the raw depth of someone's character. The beauty, tenderness, compassion, fierceness, and honesty that continue to be revealed in you are inspiring and humbling. I am constantly amazed by your grace and love for others and for our family. You are the perfect mom to Noah. You are tender and forgiving to me. You are patient and supportive of all of our wild boys. I am proud to be your husband. You are a rock and a humble leader, seeking to serve others around you. My Beauty, My Bride, My Best Friend: you are my favorite, forever and always!

APPENDIX: LIST OF ARKS

How to Use the List of Arks

A Guide for the Mental Fog

If you are reading this page first, I understand.

When you are in the thick of the "waves," your brain doesn't always work the way it used to. I remember sitting in hospital hallways and quiet living rooms, staring at pages of books I wanted to read, but the words wouldn't stick. Grief has a way of stealing your focus and leaving a heavy "mental fog" in its place.

I wrote this book to tell our story, but I created this Appendix to be your Survival Manual. Each "Ark" listed here is a condensed truth pulled from the chapters of this book. They are the foundational truths that kept our family afloat when we weren't sure we could take another breath.

Here is how I recommend using this list:

- When you are in "Extreme Triage": Don't worry about the chapters. Just scan this list. Find a sentence that resonates with your current pain and hold onto it like a life preserver.

- When you need a specific tool: If your marriage feels strained, go to the Chapter 2 Ark. If you are struggling with the silence of God, look at Part II.

- When you want to dive deeper: Each Ark is labeled with its corresponding chapter. When the fog clears enough for you to read a few pages, go to that chapter for the full story and the "why" behind the wisdom.

These aren't just quirky quotes or "feel-good" mantras. They are hard-fought anchors. They are evidence that even though the storm is real, there is a way to find passage through it.

Take what you need. Rest when you must. The Ark is holding.

Part 1: The Waves

Chapter 1 (Before the Waves): God does not always remove the storm; He provides passage through it.

Chapter 2 (Standing Together): Grief cannot be fixed, but marriage can be protected by choosing unity over winning.

Chapter 3 (Carrying the Weight): Find someone to be the communication manager for your family.

Chapter 3 (Carrying the Weight): Hope is not pretending the diagnosis isn't real; it is trusting God even when it is.

Chapter 4 (Hoarding Time): When nothing can be done, presence becomes the greatest expression of love.

Chapter 5 (The Moments After): We find true redemption not by escaping our pain, but by allowing God to lead us back to the very place where our grief began.

Chapter 5 (The Moments After): Grief marks you permanently, but it does not mean God has abandoned you.

Chapter 6 (Holding Him Until Heaven): Peace didn't remove the pain, but it carried us through it.

Chapter 7 (Even Though, We Will): The more intense our grief, the more healing our worship.

Chapter 8 (Perfect Timing): Even when we can't see it, God's timing is perfect.

Chapter 9 (The Dash): We don't solve grief, we learn to carry it by living inside the dash.

Chapter 10 (Living with Grief): The weight of our pain is matched by the depth of our love, and God meets us in the dash between them.

Chapter 11 (When Grief Has No Energy): Take a nap and learn to say No; both will be vital in this season.

Chapter 11 (When Grief Has No Energy): God is not disappointed by your limits; He designed you with them.

Chapter 12 (Birthdays Without You): Grief holds both love and absence at the same time.

Chapter 13 (A Delicate Dance): Healing is not abrupt or triumphant; it is careful and costly.

Chapter 14 (Embracing the Hard): Don't allow your grief to confuse you into thinking the easy way is the best way. Choose to do the right thing, especially when it's hard.

Chapter 14 (Embracing the Hard): Grief gives excuses to quit, but love calls us forward.

Chapter 15 (The Mercy I Didn't Expect): Carry the weight of suffering for your loved ones.

Chapter 15 (The Mercy I Didn't Expect): Both sorrow and thankfulness can be true at the same time.

Chapter 16 (Little Redeeming Moments): Redemption does not erase the darkness; it enters it.

Chapter 17 (A Testimony of Trust): Acknowledge every member of your family, including those in Heaven, when sharing your story with others.

Chapter 17 (A Testimony of Trust): Continuing to live is not a betrayal; it is a testimony.

Chapter 18 (A T-Shirt is Worth a Thousand Words): God may not remove the flood, but He never leaves the boat.

Part 2: The Foundational Ground

Chapter 19 (When God Doesn't Explain Himself): Faith rests on God's character, not on resolved explanations.

Chapter 20 (Living With the Question): Faith is faithful before and after the outcome.

Chapter 21 (The Table God Prepares): Peace is finding rest in the confidence of God's redemption.

Chapter 21 (The Table God Prepares): With Jesus, our pain creates seats at our table for goodness and mercy.

Chapter 22 (The Foundational Ark): Jesus is the only ground on which you can stand to truly navigate your grief.

Chapter 23 (Avoid the Void): Healing begins where avoidance ends.

Part 3: The Community Manual

Chapter 24 (Borrowed Strength): Letting others help is an act of grace, for them and for you.

Chapter 25 (Hurting, Healing, Helping): Health comes from honoring every season, not skipping them.

Chapter 26 (Empathy: A tool I didn't want): True empathy honors someone's pain by listening before speaking.

Chapter 27 (Questions to Avoid): Grief does not need interpretation, but needs companionship.

AUTHOR BIO

Matthew Efird is a grieving father, a husband, and a leader who has learned that true strength is not found in self-sufficiency but in a desperate need for a Savior. A graduate of The University of Georgia, Matthew and his high school sweetheart, Hannah, live outside of Athens, where they run several businesses and serve their community. Matthew is the host of the Pillars of Purpose Podcast, where he explores living a life of purpose in faith, family, and business.

Following the Trisomy 13 diagnosis and passing of their second son, Noah, Matthew felt an intense calling to share their raw journey, a path marked by both weeping and worshiping. He and his wife are the founders of Even Though, We Will, an organization dedicated to providing "Arks" of practical support and care packages to families navigating the devastating waters of a terminal diagnosis. Matthew is the proud father of four amazing boys: three who fill his home with wild joy and one who awaits him in the presence of their Savior.

STAY IN TOUCH!

Listen to a conversation Hannah and I had on the podcast about Noah's life.

Do you know someone who you would like to nominate to receive a Noah's Ark? Please submit their information here.